# What Every Catholic Should Know

## A. J. Gary

WESTBOW
PRESS
A DIVISION OF THOMAS NELSON
& ZONDERVAN

Scripture quotations marked (NRSV) are taken from the New Revised Standard Version Bible: Catholic Edition, copyright 1989, 1993, Division of Christian Education of the National Council of the Churches of Christ in the United States of America. Used by permission. All rights reserved.

Scripture quotations marked (NKJV) are taken from the New King James Version. Copyright 1979, 1980, 1982 by Thomas Nelson, Inc. Used by permission. All rights reserved.

Scripture quotations marked (TLB) are taken from The Living Bible copyright © 1971. Used by permission of Tyndale House Publishers, Inc., Carol Stream, Illinois 60188. All rights reserved.

WestBow Press books may be ordered through booksellers or by contacting:

WestBow Press
A Division of Thomas Nelson & Zondervan
1663 Liberty Drive
Bloomington, IN 47403
www.westbowpress.com
1 (866) 928-1240

ISBN: 978-1-4908-8756-2 (sc)
ISBN: 978-1-4908-8757-9 (e)

Print information available on the last page.

WestBow Press rev. date: 07/31/2015

# Dedication

My greatest desire is to see those lost in the
confusion of the Catholic religion,
brought into the light of
God's Eternal Truth.

I lovingly dedicate this book
to my brother David.

# Contents

# Acknowledgements

I wish to thank my husband for his support and advice.
Without him, this book would not have been written.

I also wish to express my appreciation to
Ann & Mark, Mary & Jim and Rose & Wayne.
Their help in providing information and
advice has been indispensable.
Thank you all!

In addition I would like to extend my gratitude
to Joe for his work in the editing of this book.

I am also grateful to Paula for her selfless act
of retyping this entire book for reprinting.

# Introduction

The Roman Catholic Church is certainly one of the largest Christian churches in existence today. The teachings of the church are derived from the church's historical tradition. Because it is so widely accepted, the <u>tradition</u> is often used as the basis of one's devotion as a Catholic. Catholic individuals put their faith in Catholicism, believing it teaches God's truth.

One of the teachings of the church is that the Bible is truly the Word of God. Therefore, I will compare Catholic teachings with Holy Scripture. Each doctrine of the church will be assessed in the light of Biblical teaching.

I challenge those who wish to know the truth to read this and compare for themselves, the Bible and Catholic doctrine. This book is not written to condemn anyone, but only to enlighten those who read it, and to show what God's Word has to say about Catholicism. If you do not wish to believe it, then I would challenge you to search for the truth on your own.

My research for this book includes the use of books and materials approved by the Roman Catholic Church, including a Catechism and the Catholic Bible. My knowledge of Catholic teachings is limited to what I have been told and what I have read. If any statement mentioned is inconsistent with Catholic doctrine, it is because it has been difficult for me to determine which beliefs are obligatory and which are dogmatic.

There is a tremendous amount of literature to study in order to understand exactly what Catholic theology teaches. Therefore, it is impossible to pinpoint all of the false teachings of the church. I will, however, attempt to focus on the key areas of Catholic teaching and thus make my purpose as clear as possible.

# Preface

C-A-T-H-O-L-I-C . . . I can see myself writing out the letters carefully. My penmanship was not very good, so I worked at it slowly. I was attending Sacred Heart Parochial School, and throughout my elementary years, I grew up thinking and living the life of a Catholic.

Sunday Mass: usually I went with Dad. He went to the early Mass that did not have a choir. It was a shorter service. Sometimes though, I would go on Saturday to the four o'clock Mass. That way I would do whatever I wanted on Sunday morning – like sleep. This Mass was convenient for Mom too, because it gave her more time to prepare the big Sunday dinner.

As I matured, I began to dislike Church. I had now entered public high school, which meant that I would have to attend C.C.D. classes. These classes taught the Catholic Doctrine to children to prepare them for the various sacraments. I could now receive the sacrament of Confirmation, after which my parents felt I would be mature enough to make my own decisions regarding "religion". With my Confirmation complete, I was now on my own.

"Great!" I used to think; "Now I can do what I want." Sunday was <u>my</u> day. No more church for me, no more confession, no more communion — just me and the Lord. I was sure God wanted it that way. I did not need church!

That attitude didn't last long though, because while half of my family attended Catholic Church, the rest were becoming involved in a Protestant church. After numerous invitations to attend a service, I finally decided to accept, and so I made my first visit to this new and unique church. "What a difference" I thought. People were so friendly, just like a real family. Immediately I became a welcomed member of that family. "Wow! This is not like Sacred Heart", I would say to myself.

Soon I was caught up in this church's activities, and I gave my total commitment to Christ, accepting Him as my personal Savior. I was also baptized as a proclamation of faith, just as Jesus instructed.

So whatever became of Sacred Heart Church? Oh, I thought about it once in a while. It did, however, start to affect me spiritually when I would study the Scriptures and read something that contradicted what I had been taught as a Catholic. I continued to store those contradictions in the back of my mind. What I did not realize was that I was building a monster of resentment towards the Catholic Church. "How could they teach me those things?" I would recall. Yet, they did and would continue to do so with other elementary grade students.

I remember one of the nuns telling us that she had married Jesus. She even showed us her wedding ring. Another nun, when speaking of Baptism, said that unless babies were baptized, they would go to hell. I was taught that only good people went to heaven. Logically that sounded right, so I tried hard to be good. Even then I had inner conflicts with the teachings of the Catholic Church.

I could never understand how I could possibly be good enough for heaven. When I was bad, I remember Mom saying, "Do you want Jesus to cry on the cross?" That was effective all right. I could not bear to think of Jesus suffering on the cross and then crying because I was disobedient. I realize now that Mom was just trying to do her best.

How about when I lost something? "Pray to Saint Anthony, he will help you find it," I was told.

I never did understand the Rosary. I figured it was a neat way of keeping track of your prayers. We would always say it on long trips, and I remember how we used to take turns saying the decades. It never sounded much like a prayer though. We had all learned to say it so fast that the "Hail Mary's" and "Holy Mary's" became a low, mumbling hum. These discrepancies became stored up offenses in my mind.

Even after becoming a Christian, I was approached with scripturally incorrect Catholic theology. My younger sister was attending C.C.D. classes one Sunday. Because I drove her to the school, I decided to stay and wait to take her home. Sitting in on the sixth and seventh grade class, I listened to the teacher discuss the upcoming visit of the Pope. You cannot imagine how astonished I was when she told these young children, "The Pope is the closest one to God." That was the breaking point in that monster of animosity in my mind. From that time on, I began to ridicule the Catholic Church, mostly to myself, but gradually to others.

My resentment became an unsettled bitterness that kept me angry against that church. During that time, my parents still remained devout Catholics, even though most of my family were becoming "born again" in Christ and entering Protestant churches.

It was at this time that I fell in love and became engaged. During my first years of marriage, I put aside those feelings. I was too busy with the thoughts of my wonderful husband and our marriage to think about Catholic teaching.

It would not end there however, again those angry thoughts returned even worse than before. Yet, during this time, something was happening to Mom. As I would talk to her, I noticed something different about her. Also, she was reading her Bible and speaking more of the Lord and of His goodness. Mom had no doubt become a true Christian, born again. "Why then, is she still Catholic?" I wondered. I was excited to hear her speak of the Lord working in her life, "but what about the Catholic fallacies?" I questioned. Mom was different than she had been when I was a youngster. The Lord was vivid in her life now more than ever. It was not so much that she was serving the church, like helping at bingo and bazaars, now I saw her serving the Lord.

It was hard for me not to question her beliefs in the Catholic Church, but I did not want to offend her. After all, I knew she had accepted Christ as her Savior, so why should I bother? I became more and more uneasy however, so I decided to say something. I brought up points about some of her church beliefs not being Biblical. I hoped she would understand, but her questions and excuses frustrated me. I could not seem to get through to her.

As I continued to discuss with her the unBiblical aspects of the Catholic Church, I realized that I lacked substantial knowledge of God's Word. I did not know enough about the truth to help Mom see it for herself.

I prayed about the problem I was facing, and God gave me the inspiration to write this book. I believe His challenge to me is two-fold. First, to bring me to a greater knowledge of His Word, and second, to remove my anger toward the Catholic Church and begin a mission to bring Catholics into the light of God's Eternal Truth.

# – 1 –

# Baptism

"Unless the baby is baptized, he will not go to heaven," Sister said.

"But what if the baby dies before they get a chance?" uttered a classmate.

"Well, sometimes the doctor involved will take water and perform an emergency baptism. Yet, even if this is not possible, if the mother just wishes that the baby be baptized, then God will accept that," Sister explained.

Again, a curious classmate pursued the question, "What if the mother does not wish it?"

"Well then," Sister continued, "the baby will end up in hell, but so will the mother, for she must be punished for preventing her child from going to heaven."

"Boy! That's pretty serious", I thought. Even as a sixth grader, I pondered the veracity of Sister's word.

As stated in a book of the history of the Catholic Church, a child must be baptized with water, "For by baptism, we are spiritually born again".

The Bible states in John 3:5, *"No one can enter the kingdom of God without being born of water and Spirit."* (NRSV) This is simply saying that we must be born not only of the flesh or womb(water), but also in the Spirit. Baptism is the action we take as Christians to reveal our faith. By being submerged in water, we symbolize our death to sin and come from the water pure, as Jesus was at His resurrection. The actual baptism in the Spirit is an inner action. It takes place when we make a conscious decision to follow Christ.

How then can a baby be baptized, when he is not yet at the age of understanding? A baby is not capable of making the decision to follow Christ, so he could not be ready to take the action of baptism. Nowhere in the Bible is it mentioned that a baby was or had to be baptized.

Christ, when speaking of baptism, meant that only those who received Him as their Savior would obtain the Holy Spirit. He also proposes that through baptism, we are testifying to His saving grace, and we are given the gift of the Holy Spirit. A great example in the Bible is found in Acts 8:34-40 where Phillip meets an Ethiopian eunuch and explains the Scriptures to him, teaching him the gospel. When the eunuch accepts Jesus as Lord and Savior he wants to be baptized. Verses 36 and 37 say *"Now as they went down the road, they came to some water. And the eunuch said, "See, here is water. What hinders me from being baptized?" Then Philip said, "If you believe with all your heart, you may."And he answered and said, "I believe that Jesus Christ is the Son of God' "* (NKJV)

Baptism is an action by someone who already accepted Christ and therefore must be old enough to understand the Gospel. A baby is not old enough to make a decision about Christ.

The Catholic Catechism states, "Baptism is the sacrament in which Jesus sends us His spirit who frees us from sin". Why then does a baby need baptism? A baby does not even know sin.

Again, Catholic teaching brings up "original sin" which, according to the Catechism, is the "sin of our first parents – because of it, we are born without sanctifying grace." In other words, because of the original sin at birth, we do not have the necessary grace to enter heaven. This is why I was taught that an un-baptized baby would go to hell. Some teachings, however, note that the un-baptized babies end up in "limbo", which is nice, but not exactly heaven. Limbo is not mentioned in the Bible, nor does apostolic teaching support it.

We are born into this world innocent of wrong doing, but because of original sin, we are born with a sin nature. Sin nature is what causes us to sin. Because of it, we cannot escape sin. For this reason, we are all sinners in need of a savior. Babies, however, are too young to understand what it is, and are incapable of making a decision to accept Christ as their Savior. This is why their Baptism can have no saving affect on them.

3

The child is, in God's eyes, pure; and if he died, would go to Heaven.

In Matthew 18:3, we read, *"Unless you change and become like children, you will never enter the kingdom of heaven."* (NRSV) Here, Jesus is telling us to become like little children. Can anyone honestly believe that these little children would not *get into the kingdom of heaven*? Christ plainly states just the opposite and goes on further to tell us to become like the little children.

In Matthew 19:14, Jesus reiterates this statement by telling His disciples, *"Let the little children come to me, and do not stop them; for it is to such as these that the kingdom of heaven belongs."* (NRSV) Children are in no need of baptism or anything like it to enter heaven. Christ said that they are already of the kingdom of heaven.

It is only when a child is at the age of reasoning that he is subject to the punishment of hell. We cannot specifically decide what that age is, but we are all responsible for the Christian examples we are to be. It is through this example and proper upbringing that a child will come to accept Christ at a young age.

John 1:33, refers to Christ baptizing with the Holy Spirit. *"He..is the one who baptizes with the Holy Spirit."* (NRSV) This spiritual baptism takes place when a person receives Jesus as their Savior. The submersion in water is only one's outward act of obedience to God. It **symbolizes** one's cleansing by the Holy Spirit. It is the union with Christ and the receiving of the Spirit that brings one to salvation, not the symbolic act of being baptized with water.

In Mark 1:8, John the Baptist says *"I have baptized you with water; but he* (Jesus) *will baptize you with the Holy Spirit."* (NRSV) The baptism of the Holy Spirit is the true baptism. John knew this and demonstrated the need for repentance using the act of water baptism as a symbol.

I believe that Baptism is important, and that it is commanded of a new believer. The type of baptizing that takes place in the Bible is not a "sprinkling" with water. In fact, the word baptize is derived from the Greek word "baptizo", which means "to make whelmed (i.e., fully wet)" and "to cover wholly with a fluid". This is very different from the Catholic way of baptizing, with the sprinkling of water on the baby's head. The act of submerging the Christian under the water symbolizes the death and burial of the flesh and as the believer comes out of the water it characterizes the resurrection of new life in Christ. The Biblical baptism is very different from the Catholic baptism and it is clear in Scripture that the purpose of Baptism is not what the Catholic church teaches.

# – 2 –

# The Eucharist

"Now remember", Sister told us, "this is an important day. Today you will receive Jesus for the first time. And do not forget, Jesus' body is in the Eucharist, so do not chew it!"

"Gee! He must be awfully small", I contemplated silently. I then went on to receive my first Holy Communion. Did I feel different? No, I did not feel any change, even though this was such a big spiritual event. I did, however, enjoy all the attention given to me as only a second grader. My parents and the other people in the church looked at my classmates and me with such importance.

The Eucharist, according to the Catholic Church's basic Catechism, is "A sacrament, <u>a sacrifice</u>, and the abiding presence of Jesus Himself, God and Man." It teaches that the "Last Supper" is the basis for their sacrament of the Eucharist. It also states, as I have underlined, that it is a sacrifice.

The Catechism Scripture reference is from Luke

22:19-20, *"Then he took a loaf of bread, and when he had given thanks, he broke it and gave it to them, saying, "This is my body, which is given for you. Do this in remembrance of me." And he did the same with the cup after supper, saying, "This cup that is poured out for you is the new covenant in my blood"* (NRSV)

Catholic teaching states that when saying this, Christ meant that He would die for us each time we partake in the meal or communion.

Another verse in Scripture used by Catholics to explain Christ's bodily presence in the bread is John 6:53-58, Christ tells those listening, *"Those who eat my flesh and drink my blood abide in me, and I in them."* (NRSV) Also, in John 6:51, Christ calls himself *"Living Bread"*.

Looking at these verses apart from the whole of Scripture can lead to numerous interpretations. This is why it is important to study verses within the context to see what they really mean.

To begin we must come to understand the significance of the Last Supper. This dinner was a Passover meal that Jesus shared with His disciples. The Passover meal was celebrated by the Jews as a remembrance that God "passed over" them when He took the lives of the first-born sons of the Egyptians. In Exodus 12:11-13, God speaks to the people of Israel, *"I will pass over you, and no plague shall destroy you when I strike the land of Egypt."* (NRSV) This celebration of the Passover was in thanksgiving of God's mercy on them. All those who put the blood of the lamb on their doorpost were spared from God's angel of death. At Passover, a lamb is slain and served as a reminder of the blood of the lamb that saved their household.

First Corinthians 5:7, says that Christ is our Passover Lamb who was slain for our sins. *"For indeed Christ, our Passover, was sacrificed for us."* (NKJV) Just as God saved the people of Israel from the slaying in Egypt, He would also save us through Christ's death. We are told in Isaiah 53, of God's promise to send a Messiah. In verse 7, reference is made to the Messiah as having been a lamb led to the slaughter.

Well now, by looking at that verse again, Luke 22:19-20, we can understand what Christ really meant. He showed by the breaking of the bread how He soon would be broken, and that the pouring of the cup was just like the pouring of His blood for our salvation. Jesus always used analogies and parables in His teachings. Here He was again using an analogy to describe His death.

It is also important to point out that it was the **shedding of the blood**, not the eating of the lamb that saved them from death. Likewise, the shedding of Jesus blood saves us, not eating His flesh.

In John 6:53-58, where Christ states, "eat my flesh", He again is using symbolism. This is confirmed by His statement just a few verses later in 63, where He says, *"It is the spirit that gives life; the flesh is useless. The words that I have spoken to you are spirit and life."* (NRSV) Christ was indicating that it is not His physical body that He wants us to eat, but that His words are a spiritual food necessary for life — eternal life. It is symbolic, not actual.

To continue, in John 6:51, Christ is called *"Living Bread"*. If we were to understand this as a literal statement, then we would also have to believe that Christ is physically a *lamb*, as stated in 1 Corinthians 5:7 or *living water* (John 4:14) or a *door* (John 10:7-9), or a *vine* (John 15:5). These are all metaphors describing Christ and His attributes. Unfortunately, when taken out of context, it fits conveniently into the Catholic teaching of the Eucharist.

The Bible explicitly teaches that Christ was referring to Himself as symbolic bread. He uses this symbol of bread to teach His disciples about His death. By taking this as a literal statement and asserting that Christ is somehow mysteriously transformed into actual bread, is nothing but misinterpretation.

The second aspect of the Eucharist that is contrary to Biblical belief is that Christ is renewing His sacrifice in this sacrament. The Catechism teaches that this sacrifice of Christ continually takes place at each Mass. The Bible, on the other hand, teaches otherwise.

First and foremost, Christ says, *"Do this in remembrance of me."* He was giving a new meaning to the Passover celebration. Now, instead of looking on that meal as a memorial of the original Passover, He is giving us a new reason for celebration. Just like the Passover meal eaten by the Jews years ago, Christ

9

instituted a new meal to be <u>symbolic</u>, and as a memorial of His death. Similar to the way our Thanksgiving meal commemorates the first harvest of the original pilgrims at Plimoth Plantation.

This celebration of communion reminds us of Christ's sacrifice. It was not intended to be a repetition of the sacrifice. This doctrine supposes that Christ is being crucified again and again.

Yet, the Bible teaches us very clearly that "re-crucifying" Christ is not necessary and is even impossible.

In Hebrews 10:10-12, we read *"And it is by God's will that we have been sanctified through the offering of the body of Jesus Christ once for all. And every priest stands day after day at his service, offering again and again the same sacrifices that can never take away sins. But when Christ had offered for all time a single sacrifice for sins, "he sat down at the right hand of God."* (NRSV)

In this passage, the writer of Hebrews is explaining that Christ has paid the price for our sins. He talks about how years earlier God's people needed to purge their sins by having a priest sacrifice their offering. This ritual took place day after day, as the people continued to sin. God had instituted this sacrificial offering as a way to keep His people in submission. However, it did not have any real saving power. That is why it took the perfection of Christ to be the ultimate sacrifice.

The writer also states that Christ's sacrifice was sufficient for <u>all people</u> for <u>all time</u>. Christ died <u>once</u> as a sacrifice and that took care of all sin. To say that He must renew this sacrifice in the act of the Eucharist is contradicting Hebrews 10.

In addition to the verses from Hebrews, we read in Romans 6:9, that Christ's sacrifice renewed is impossible. It says, *"We know that Christ, being raised from the dead, will never die again; death no longer has dominion over him."* (NRSV) Without His death there is no sacrifice, so according to this passage, Christ could not perform another sacrifice.

Also, in Hebrews 6:4-6, we are told, *"For it is impossible to restore again to repentance those who have once been enlightened,. . . and then have fallen away, since on their own they are crucifying again the Son of God and are holding him up to contempt."* (NRSV) This distinctly confirms that Christ cannot be crucified again.

Hebrews 10:12, stated previously, *"He sat down . . . at the right hand of God."* Christ is sitting at the right hand of the Father. He is not present physically in the Eucharist, as Catholic teaching contends.

Another aspect of this sacrifice that shows its error is also found in the Catechism. It states: "Christ renews the sacrifice of the cross in the Mass, in an un-bloody manner, for our sake."

We have already seen clearly in the above Scripture references that Christ had only to die **once**, and that it would not only be unnecessary, but impossible for Him to die again. However, this suggestion of a sacrifice in an un-bloody manner continues to deepen Catholic error in this teaching. It says in Hebrew 9:22, *"Indeed, under* *the law almost everything is purified with blood, and without the shedding of blood there is no forgiveness of sins."* (NRSV) Here we are told that Christ's blood was shed for us, specifically because blood in a sacrifice was necessary for forgiveness. Yet, if the original sacrifice at Calvary was not enough and must be performed over and over at each Mass, what good can an un-bloody sacrifice do? According to the epistle of Hebrews – nothing!

The Eucharist is taught to be the actual body and blood of Christ. Although some Catholics may believe it is a symbol, the church mandates that during what is called transubstantiation, the elements of bread and wine become Christ's physical body and blood.

In Acts 15:20, we are told to *"abstain from . . . blood"*, referring to its consumption. How then can we believe Jesus would want us to drink His blood? Here is just another example of fault in the Eucharist teachings.

Ultimately, the sacrament of the Eucharist, as the Catholic Church teaches it, only serves to ensnare Catholic parishioners into believing that they need to go to Mass in order to keep Christ inside themselves. But what is communion really about?

The tradition of communion began with the apostles and disciples of Christ. They were the first to partake in communion, and taught others of its significance. If anyone knew what communion was about it would be these followers of Christ.

The book of Acts records the beginnings of Christ's church. In Acts 2:40-46 and 20:7, communion is referred to as *"breaking bread"*, not partaking of Christ's body. Acts 2:42 *"They devoted themselves to the apostles' teaching and fellowship, to the breaking of bread and the prayers."* (NRSV) And Acts 20:7 *"On the first day of the week, when we met to break bread."* (NRSV)

First Corinthians 11:25, states that He *"took the cup"*. This passage makes no mention of wine or its transition into blood. Verse 26, continues, *"For as often as you eat this bread and drink the cup, you proclaim the Lord's death until he comes."* (NRSV) Here we can see that there is no mention of the body and blood of Christ, but only the elements of the bread and the cup. If transubstantiation had occurred, these would certainly have been referred to as "body" and "blood" of Christ, but only the elements of the bread and the cup are mentioned. Also, it states that this act of communion proclaims the Lord's death not "repeats" it. The word "proclaim" specifically means to "testify" or "speak of" something. By taking communion, we are making known the death of Christ, which we are thankful for because it is the source of our salvation.

The apostles did take communion on a regular basis; how often is unknown. They did teach that the breaking of bread was part of the church's responsibility. This act, however, was not instituted to have a saving effect on Christians. Its primary purpose was to cause Christians to recognize again the sacrifice Christ made for them.

The apostles carried on what Jesus taught them. They celebrated communion as a thanksgiving to Christ. They did not teach what Catholic theology teaches about communion. In fact, it wasn't until the 12th Century that the idea of transubstantiation (the actual presence of Christ in the Eucharist) was made a doctrine of the church. Over a thousand years had passed since Christ's death, and the teachings of the apostles had changed drastically. The truth, nevertheless, remains in the example that the apostles maintained. Their illustration of the Lord's Supper is what Christ intended; in remembrance of Him and as a memorial to Him.

Ultimately, the teaching of the Eucharist has instituted a form of idolatry. When a Catholic parishioner enters the church he will genuflect, or bow, toward the sanctuary where the Eucharist is kept. This act is meant to be in reverence to Jesus who they believe is actually present in the elements of bread and wine. Similar to the idol worshippers in the Old Testament who bowed down to man-made gods, Catholics who put their trust in the bread and wine are giving their worship to lifeless items. As stated in Isaiah 2:8 "... *Their land is filled with idols; they bow down to the work of their hands, to what their own fingers have made."* (NRSV)

The bread and wine are not the actual flesh and blood of Jesus. Catholics who believe in transubstantiation and the physical presence of Christ in the Eucharist are putting their faith in the man-made teachings of the church and not God's Word. This misdirected faith has lead many Catholics to believe that they **need** to receive Communion regularly in order to be filled with Christ. However, Jesus has told us in His Word in Matthew

28:20 *"And remember, I am with you always, to the end of the age."* (NRSV)

When we accept Jesus into our hearts He comes to live inside us. That's why 2 Corinthians 6:16 states *"For we are the temple of the living God."* (NRSV) We embody the Spirit of Christ; and with Him living through us there is no need for us to take Him in continually.

If we want to be close to Christ we only need to spend time with Him. We commune with God through prayer and reading His Word and He enlightens us through the Holy Spirit inside us. Believing that we need to receive the Eucharist in order to somehow be filled with Christ is a sad conviction. In many ways, it constrains our relationship with God, diminishing the Father–child bond that Jesus came to establish.

Romans 8: 14-16; *"For all who are led by the Spirit of God are children of God. For you did not receive a spirit of slavery to fall back into fear, but you have received a spirit of adoption. When we cry, "Abba! Father!" it is that very Spirit bearing witness with our spirit that we are children of God."* (NRSV)

I pray that if you are putting your faith in the sacrament of the Eucharist, you will allow God to show you in His Word the truth; and put your faith in the single sacrifice Jesus made over 2000 years ago.

# – 3 –

# Confirmation

"To be ready to receive this sacrament, you must perform free-will chores", Sister began. "Helping the elderly or other good deeds are acceptable", she said. "Hmmm, ten hours of good deeds", I mused, "What can I do?"

My final goal as a Catholic was to be confirmed. Not because I felt a need for it, but because my parents did. They reasoned that once confirmed, I would be ready to make my own decision about church. I wasn't even sure what Confirmation was about, but I knew it was all I needed to finally be "on my own".

"The Holy Spirit comes to us in a special way", is how the Catholic Catechism explains Confirmation. In this sacrament, the Bishop gives a blessing to the participants, thus, sending in the Holy Spirit.

Receiving the Holy Spirit is an important issue in the Bible. The act of Confirmation, however, is not found in Scripture. By carefully studying God's Word, we can find out just how to receive this third Person of the Trinity.

In Matthew 3:11, John the Baptist tells of his baptizing with water, but when Christ comes, *"He will baptize you with the Holy Spirit."* (NRSV) Jesus did perform this type of baptism on the day of Pentecost.

Before Christ's death and resurrection, His followers were baptized in water to show that they had turned from their sin. Jesus promised that He would send His Spirit once He was gone. The Bible says in John 14:15-17, *"If you love me, you will keep my commandments. And I will ask the Father, and he will give you another Advocate, to be with you forever. This is the Spirit of truth"* (NRSV) Jesus tells His disciples that they will not be left alone. He assures them of the Holy Spirit's imminent arrival.

This indwelling of the Holy Spirit is an important part of a Christian's future. Christ told of the Spirit's purpose John 14:26, *"the Holy Spirit, whom the Father will send in my name, will teach you everything, and remind you of all that I have said to you."* (NRSV) Here we see the importance of the Holy Spirit as a guide to us. It is through Him that we can understand the Bible.

All that Jesus taught about the Holy Spirit took place on Pentecost. The apostles were filled with the Holy Spirit and were able to speak other languages. This made them confident to preach the gospel, no longer fearing the opposition. The Holy Spirit had given them power that came from God.

This is why this type of Baptism was such an integral

part of the Christian life and still is today. The Holy Spirit gives us the ability to do God's will. He is also the One who convicts us when we sin. The Bible says in John 16:8, *"And when He has come, He will convict the world of sin, and of righteousness, and of judgment"* (NKJV)

The importance of the Holy Spirit is evident in these verses of Scripture, but now let us see how the disciples acquired this gift from God.

As recorded in Acts 2:38, Peter is speaking to the crowd with the other apostles. They had just received the Holy Spirit. The crowd they were preaching to started to believe in Jesus. When the people asked what they should do, Peter said, *"Repent, and be baptized every one of you in the name of Jesus Christ so that your sins may be forgiven; and you will receive the gift of the Holy Spirit."* (NRSV) This simple act of faith, turning away from sin and believing in Christ, resulted in the forgiveness of sin and the manifestation of the Holy Spirit.

The sacrament of Confirmation is a ritual that is conducted without necessity. The Holy Spirit comes to us when we take the appropriate action as seen above. No man has the ability to impute the Holy Spirit in someone else. Peter clearly states that the responsibility belonged to the sinner and that the gifts were promised thereafter. Peter did not administer a blessing on those who took this step. He simply told them what would happen. The gifts were received by all those who obeyed God's Word. It was not Peter or any of the other apostles that activated the Holy Spirit to come into these penitents.

Anyone can receive the gift of the Holy Spirit today, just as simply as it was years ago. Not through the act of a sacrament such as Confirmation, but through a personal commitment to Christ, by turning away from sin and turning to God.

# − 4 −

# Penance

"Bless me Father, for I have sinned", I began to recite again to myself the prayer of Penance. "I sure hope I don't mess up," I thought while trying to memorize the words.

As I sat in church, my mind was tuned only to that prayer, even though Sister was giving last minute instructions. "Ask God to help you remember all of your sins so you will know what to ask forgiveness for," she said lastly.

One by one my classmates entered the confessional. I wondered just what it was like behind that curtain. "Oh, I'm next!" I realized, and on I went to receive the sacrament of penance for the first time.

"Bless me Father . . .," I began nervously, and continued through the entire prayer finishing with the list of sins that had come to my mind. This first confession was quite awkward for me. I was not comfortable telling my sins to a stranger behind a dark screen. Each subsequent confession was no more comfortable than the one before. I felt it was probably meant to be that way, considering it was a sacrament dealing with sin. Nevertheless, I did not like going to confession, nor did I truly understand the purpose.

After each confession my sins were absolved, and I was given my "penance". The penance was a prayer or series of prayers that I had to recite at the front of the church.

Penance is, according to the Catechism, "something done or accepted to make up for sin." Catholics are told to confess their sins to a priest because he has to know what our sins are in order to forgive them in Christ's name.

Forgiveness is the key element to this sacrament. The main purpose of penance is to be "set free from sin, from its eternal punishment, and from at least some of its temporal punishment."

According to Catholic teaching, John 20:22-23, verifies that Christ gave only the apostles the power to forgive sins. It also concludes that priests are the "only true successors" of the apostles and are allowed to forgive man's sins. In these verses of Scripture, Jesus says, *"Receive the Holy Spirit. If you forgive the sins of any, they are forgiven them; if you retain the sins of any, they are retained."* (NRSV)

Here Jesus specifically uses the <u>past tense</u> in saying that they "are forgiven". He does not say they "will be forgiven." In other words, Jesus was saying that if you forgive anyone his sins, they have <u>already been forgiven</u>. The forgiveness of man has already been established through Christ and is attained by the acceptance of

Him as Savior. The power that was handed out here by Christ, was the privilege to assure others of their forgiveness if they accept Christ, or assure them of their lack of forgiveness if they reject Him.

Secondly, this statement from Christ was not spoken to the apostles alone. Verse 19 of the same chapter states that it was when *"the disciples were together"* that this was spoken. The disciples or learners were the many followers of Christ. They were unlike the apostles who were specifically chosen by Jesus. In fact, not even all the apostles were there. Verse 24, tells us that Thomas was absent at this meeting.

The group that is represented in this assembly is comprised of various men and women who were followers of Christ, not just the apostles.

This is important because Catholicism teaches that the priest alone has the power to forgive sins. This is because it claims that priests are the only true successors of the apostles. Well, if such power to forgive sins was given, then it would have been given to all those present. This, in turn, would then have to transmit the same authority to every Christian today. Certainly this is not supported by Catholic teaching, yet it would logically have to apply because of who the group was that Jesus spoke to.

The truth is, that the Bible leaves the power of forgiveness in heaven. It is not our right to forgive others for God. Our privilege is that we can tell the sinner how he can gain forgiveness from God.

Another aspect of penance that is unbiblical is the practice of the penance itself. The Catechism explains that by doing an act of penance one can "make up" for their sin. This is totally against God's purpose in Christ. As was mentioned in the chapter on the Eucharist, Jesus paid the price <u>in full</u> for the sins of the world. By trying to make up for our sin on our own, we are claiming that Jesus didn't cleanse us completely. We are saying that His sacrifice wasn't enough.

First John 1:9 states, *"If we confess our sins, he who is faithful and just will forgive us our sins and cleanse us from all unrighteousness."* (NRSV) This statement explains God's method for us to attain forgiveness. Unlike the Catholic confession, we are told to confess to "Him". An earthly "priest" is of no use in the matter of God's plan for our forgiveness.

Other passages from Scripture that explain God's forgiveness include Acts 10:43, *"Everyone who believes in him receives forgiveness of sins."* (NRSV); Acts 26:18 says that through Jesus forgiveness is proclaimed, and Ephesians 1:7, *"in Him (Jesus) we have - forgiveness."* (NRSV)

Christ is the source of forgiveness. He made it possible for us to receive forgiveness without the need for an act of "penance". We are not told to make up for our sin.

Hebrews 10:10, states *"And it is by God's will that we have been sanctified through the offering of the body of Jesus Christ once for all."* (NRSV) Christ then, made the only necessary sacrifice to pay for all our sins – past, present and future. Hebrews 10:14 continues, *"For by a single offering he has perfected for all time those who are sanctified,"* (NRSV) So God sees us as being perfect. No longer do we have to pay for our sins because the one act of Christ's death is still in effect. Notice how the verse uses the present tense, *"those who are sanctified".* In other words, the saving power of His sacrifice is continually at work. Our part in receiving the forgiveness is to confess with a repentant heart. If we are honestly sorry for our offense, then we can accept His immediate forgiveness because the penalty has already been paid.

Catholicism teaches that "Jesus died to make up for the offenses of our first parents' sin and our own personal sins. But more than that, He died so that we have a chance of reaching the happiness of heaven." The Catechism is right in saying that Christ died to save us from sin, but not that we "may have a chance" of reaching heaven. Jesus' death made it possible for us to be **guaranteed** everlasting life, if we believe and accept Him.

Receiving the gift of salvation doesn't mean we suddenly stop sinning. We continue as Christians to be tempted, however, now with Christ in our hearts, we have the power of the Holy Spirit to overcome temptation. The Bible says in 1 Corinthians 10:13, *"No testing has overtaken you that is not common to everyone. God is faithful, and he will not let you be tested beyond your strength, but with the testing he will also provide the way out so that you may be able to endure it."* (NRSV)

If, as Christians, we do fall into our old nature and sin, then we must confess those sins to God. Through Christ, we will be forgiven and we will be given the strength to battle against the attacks of Satan. In addition to the power to overcome sin, the Holy Spirit also convicts us of sin. The sense of remorse we feel keeps us from desiring sin. All of these work to keep us in obedience to God.

Once our sins are forgiven, no other acts are needed. We read in Hebrews 10:18, *"Where there is forgiveness of these, there is no longer any offering for sin."* (NRSV)

Jesus said it best as He was dying on the cross in John 19, verse 30, *"When Jesus had received the wine, he said, "It is finished." Then he bowed his head and gave up his spirit"* (NRSV) It is finished indeed. The act of redemption was complete so there was no need for additional atonement for sin, not in an act of penance or any other work of our flesh. The sacrament of penance claims that we must pay a penalty for our sin. The Bible says differently. In fact, trying to make up for our sin insults God's faithfulness to do as He said.

# – 5 –

# Matrimony

The sacrament of marriage is a very serious subject. It is the uniting of two persons in the sight of God. There is only one element of the Catholic rite of marriage that I wish to question. That is, the establishment of annulment.

Annulment, according to the Catechism is "a degree of nullity — a decision by the church that authorizes an apparently valid marriage between two baptized persons can be declared null because of a fatal flaw," and "make the marriage, no marriage, from the start."

The act of annulment is provided to those "rare cases" of marriage with serious problems. It grants to the troubled couple a way out. It makes a claim that the marriage never even took place!

This is absolutely ridiculous. To have a valid marriage take place and then because of a problem, no matter how serious, say that the marriage did not occur, is foolish. It is like telling God that it never happened.

Matthew 19:6 states *"Therefore what God has joined*

*together, let no one separate."* (NRSV) This verse from Scripture is quoted often in books on Catholic teaching. It is used to condemn the act of divorce, but annulment is no different. It goes against the same principle indicated in the above verse.

When a couple makes the decision to join together in marriage, and they include God in their vows, they take on the responsibility of their action. The church's responsibility is only in the initial act of marrying the two. Certainly, a minister should be available to counsel the couple before they marry and also be ready to help restore a troubled marriage. But offering a "way out" of the marriage is not Biblical.

If a couple decides to end their marriage they are accountable for that choice. There is nothing in Scripture or the history of the church that even suggests such an act, acceptable by God, to end a marriage. Annulment was instituted by the Catholic church of its own accord. It is certainly not God ordained, nor is it acceptable to Him.

In one such case, a faithful Catholic woman was allowed to "annul" her marriage. This was after being married more than ten years, and after four children. The problem concerned the husband who had become an alcoholic. The claim considered that the wife was unaware of his problem and an innocent victim in the relationship. She was granted an annulment, by which the church claimed that the marriage never took place. But I would ask, what about the children? Do they not exist? This true example shows how absurd annulment is.

Even though this is not the typical case, it proves how detrimental such an act is. Annulment gives married couples an escape. But, furthermore, it allows such couples to believe that if it is okay with the Church, it is okay with God.

The Bible does talk about divorce in both the old and new testaments. In Deuteronomy 24:1, Moses had given permission for a man to divorce his wife if *"she does not please him because he finds something objectionable about her, and so he writes her a certificate of divorce..."* (NRSV) In Matthew 5:31-32 Jesus refers to this provision for divorce. He said *"It was also said, 'Whoever divorces his wife, let him give her a certificate of divorce. But I say to you that anyone who divorces his wife, except on the ground of unchastity, causes her to commit adultery,..."* (NRSV)

In Matthew 19:4-6 Jesus is talking about marriage. *"Have you not read that the one who made them at the beginning 'made them male and female,' and said, 'For this reason a man shall leave his father and mother and be joined to his wife, and the two shall become one flesh'? So they are no longer two, but one flesh. Therefore what God has joined together, let no one separate."* (NRSV) The disciples question him about this. *"Why then did Moses command us to give a certificate of dismissal and to divorce her?"* (NRSV) Jesus answers them. *"It was because you were so hard-hearted that Moses allowed you to divorce your wives, but from the beginning it was not so. And I say to you, whoever divorces his wife, except for unchastity, and marries another commits adultery."* (NRSV)

So God's Word does address the issue of divorce. Matthew 19:6 *"Therefore what God has joined together, let no one separate"* (NRSV) dictates God's will that marriages remain intact. However, Jesus, as quoted twice in Matthew, grants an exception when he says *"except for unchastity (sexual immorality)"*. So, if there is a case of adultery, God allows divorce. He does not claim "the marriage, no marriage, from the start." He simply permits the couple to obtain a divorce in the legal sense, unlike annulment which is a church instituted separation.

Annulment is a solution that the Catholic Church uses to conform to today's society. By conforming, they are giving another name to divorce and alleging it to be acceptable by God. It is not necessary to repeat Scripture concerning this. The Catholic Church uses these same verses when discussing divorce, but then they turn and offer the same solution through the act of annulment.

# – 6 –

# Prayer

"Mommy" I said, rubbing my sleepy eyes, "I had a bad dream." The usual reply came, "say three Hail Mary's." Slowly I went back to bed knowing that Mom was too sleepy to fully understand what I was going through. I whispered the "Hail Mary" as I drifted off to sleep.

What do prayers like "Hail Mary", "Glory Be", "Apostles Creed", "Act of Contrition", "Hail Holy Queen", etc., all mean? As a Catholic being taught in a Catholic school, I was always instructed to memorize each prayer of the church. I was never taught to pray on my own.

We are taught in God's Word how to pray through Christ's instruction and His disciples' example. There is no indication at all of repetitious prayer. In fact, we find in Matthew 6:7 what Jesus taught us about prayer. He said, *"When you are praying, do not heap up empty phrases as the Gentiles do; for they think that they will be heard because of their many words."* (NRSV) Here Jesus tells us not to use empty phrases over and over.

The Greek word used here is "battos" which means "vain repetition". We are told when we pray not to use "battos" or say the same prayers over and over.

Christ knew that praying this way would be futile. A prayer that is memorized is sure to become meaningless. Can anyone honestly say they have <u>always</u> put their thoughts into a prayer they have memorized? Jesus knew that this would be impossible, so He tells us not to pray this way.

The prayers of the Catholic Church are numerous and honor everyone from God and Mary the mother of Jesus, to hundreds of saints. These prayers are taught to Catholics who then memorize them and pray them over and over again.

Jesus discourages this type of prayer and says so. But He does not stop there. He went on to teach us how to pray. The Lord's Prayer is Christ's example for us to follow, however, even the "Our Father" was not meant to be recited incessantly. In Matthew 6:9-13, it states Jesus' example of how to pray. *"Our Father in Heaven,"*; begin by addressing God and His holy place. *"Hallowed be your name,"*; show Him honor and praise. *"Your kingdom come, your will be done, on earth as it is in heaven,"*; pray for God's will to be done, not your own. *"Give us this day our daily bread,"*; ask Him to supply your needs. *"And forgive us our debts as we also have forgiven our debtors"*; ask forgiveness for your sins as long as you have forgiven those who have sinned against you. *"And do not bring us to the time of trial but rescue us from the evil one,"* (NRSV) finally ask God to help you fight temptation so that you can resist sin.

When ending a prayer, we should remember that in John 14:14, Jesus said, *"If in my name you ask me for anything, I will do it".* Appropriately, we should end with "in Jesus' name we pray", and of course, "Amen" which means "so be it", which reaffirms what has just been said.

This is how we are taught to pray, not repetitiously, but from the heart. When prayers are repeated incessantly they become vain and meaningless. This fact is inevitable. We are supposed to talk to God from within ourselves. Our prayers are a conversation with Him.

In an earthly relationship, if a child asked his father for something by repeating someone else's words over and over, it would be foolish. What parent would want their child to come to them that way? It is entirely impersonal and aloof. What makes us think God would accept that kind of petition.

Therefore, we should pray as Jesus showed us; not continuously repeating prayers written by someone else. Although they may be wonderfully written, God appreciates much more our own prayers from the heart.

Additionally, Catholics are taught to pray to many different saints. <u>Sainthood in Roman Catholicism</u> online responds to the question of saints by teaching that they are "especially holy men and women who, through extraordinary lives of virtue, have already entered

Heaven". Thus, being in heaven <u>already</u>, now gives them the ability to intercede to God for us.

The apostles for example are considered saints, as are many other virtuous people. Each of these men and women were honored in the church as worthy of "sainthood" and many of them are said to be chosen as special protectors or guardians over areas of life. These patron saints include Francis of Assisi, the Patron of ecologists, Saint Christopher the Patron of Travelers, Saint Thomas Aquinas the Patron of Universities and Students, Saint Anthony the Patron of Lost Articles. According to <u>Catholic Online</u> there are over ten thousand Catholic saints and as many subjects of their patronage.

The problem with this doctrine is that it has **no** basis in Scripture and in fact goes against Biblical teaching. John 16:23-24, confirms this. Jesus tells us, *"Very truly, I tell you, if you ask anything of the Father in my name, he will give it to you. Until now you have not asked for anything in my name. Ask and you will receive, so that your joy may be complete."* (NRSV) We do not have to go to the saints to receive what we need. Jesus tells us that through Him, we will receive. This is a direct promise from Christ Himself and He tells us to go directly through Him to the Father.

Catholics maintain that they are merely asking the saints in heaven to pray for them the way they ask friends here on earth to do the same. There are two major obstacles with this belief. One is that asking a friend on earth is encouraged in the Bible but asking a "dead" person is against Biblical teaching. Leviticus 20:27 *"A man or a woman who is a medium or a wizard shall be put to death."* (NRSV) Here, we are told that speaking to the dead is an act worthy of the death penalty. The church may argue that the saints aren't "dead" but alive in Christ, however, the word dead is meant for those who have died on earth. God strictly forbids talking to anyone who has left their earthly bodies.

Secondly, there's no real proof that a saint could even hear us, and even if they could, we would have to assume that they could somehow hear thousands of people all at once. The ability of an all-hearing being can only be attributed to God, our omniscient Creator. The saints, even in heaven, are still finite beings with limitations.

Ultimately, the most dangerous part of this doctrine is the reality that it can and has led to misdirected worship. This is a quote from a Catholic who lost something and then after praying to St Anthony, found it. "I have great faith in Saint Anthony....Saint Anthony has miraculous powers....Pray to Saint Anthony and believe that the lost article will be found" If we asked a friend here on earth to pray for us, and then after talking with them had our pray answered, could we rightfully say that the friend had miraculous powers or that we had faith in that friend to have our prayers answered. Certainly not, for our faith should be in God alone and only God can perform miracles.

Even if the church states that it is to ask the saints to pray for them, the prayers themselves do not reflect this "asking a friend" principle. The following portions of prayers to St Anthony prove that saints are not just "friends" being asked for prayer.

"St. Anthony, <u>Restorer of Sight to the Blind</u>, please sharpen my spiritual vision.", "Help us <u>by your power before God</u> to be peacemakers.", "This favor <u>I ask of you in Christ's name</u>.", "Because of <u>your powerful intercession with God</u>, I am confident that <u>you will continue to assist me</u> in my daily life.", "St. Anthony, <u>Performer of Miracles, please obtain for me the blessings</u> God holds in reserve for those who serve Him"

In these prayers Anthony has been deemed a powerful intercessor with the ability to heal the blind. This implies we don't have the same status with God that these "saints" do. This belief only serves to separate us from God; making us think we are less worthy than others and giving the impression that we need to seek the help of someone "more worthy" than us. Yet the Bible clearly tells us that we can go directly to the Father through Jesus. In John 14:13, Jesus tells us, *"I will do whatever you ask in my name, so that the Father may be glorified in the Son."* (NRSV) God the Father is ready to answer our prayers; He's not giving more favor to us because we have a particular saint on our side. We have Jesus on our side and He is all we need.

When we pray to saints to help us with a special need we are attributing to these saints, special abilities.

Doing this detracts from the predominance of Jesus Christ as our divine and human mediator.

So who are the saints of the <u>Bible</u>? Romans 15:25 says *"At present, however, I am going to Jerusalem in a ministry to the saints"* (NRSV) And Romans 12:13 we are instructed in love - *"Contribute to the needs of the saints; extend hospitality to strangers.."* (NRSV) In Philippians 4:22 Paul begins his letter *"All the saints greet you, especially those of the emperor's household."* (NRSV) These are only a few of many references to the saints in the New Testament. In fact, the Bible calls <u>all those who are followers of Jesus Christ</u>, saints. In Romans 8:27 Paul tells us that the Holy Spirit makes intercession for us, *"And God, who searches the heart, knows what is the mind of the Spirit, because the Spirit intercedes for the saints according to the will of God."* (NRSV) The saints are Christians, ordinary men and women who belong to Christ. The Catholic Church has taken the word saint and "specialized" it by relegating it to a unique group of individuals.

Another issue in conjunction with prayer is the placement of statues and images throughout the church to "assist" the Catholic in prayer. I remember talking to a non-Catholic friend when I was a preteen. She had gone into a Catholic church once and saw the statues and people praying before them. She asked me why we worship statues. I told her what I had been taught in my CCD classes, "We don't worship statues we just pray to the person the statue represents." That was the standard "answer" to anyone who would question the images representing Jesus, Mary and innumerable saints within Catholic churches everywhere.

When I became a Christian I began to question this tradition in light of what I had be studying in the Bible. It was especially evident to me after reading the Ten Commandments that these statues were really a form of disobedience to God's Word.

We read in Exodus 20 verses 3 through 17 the list of commandments God gave to Moses on Mount Sinai.

Verse 3: *"You shall have no other gods before me.*

Verse 4: *You shall not make for yourself a carved image—any likeness of anything that is in heaven above, or that is in the earth beneath, or that is in the water under the earth.*

Verse 5: *you shall not bow down to them nor serve them. For I, the Lord your God, am a jealous God, visiting the iniquity of the fathers upon the children to the third and fourth generations of those who hate Me,*

Verse 6: *but showing mercy to thousands, to those who love Me and keep My commandments.*

Verse 7: *You shall not take the name of the Lord your God in vain, for the Lord will not hold him guiltless who takes His name in vain.*

Verse 8: *Remember the Sabbath day, to keep it holy.*

Verse 9: *Six days you shall labor, and do all your work,*

Verse 10: *but the seventh day is the Sabbath of the Lord your God. In it you shall do no work: you, nor your son, nor your daughter, nor your male servant, nor your female servant, nor your cattle, nor your stranger who is within your gates.*

Verse 11: *For in six days the Lord made the heavens and the earth, the sea, and all that is in them, and rested the seventh day. Therefore the Lord blessed the Sabbath day and hallowed it.*

Verse 12: *Honor your father and your mother, that your days may be long upon the land which the Lord your God is giving you.*

Verse 13: *You shall not murder.*

Verse 14: *You shall not commit adultery.*

Verse 15: *You shall not steal.*

Verse 16: *You shall not bear false witness against your neighbor.*

Verse 17: *You shall not covet your neighbor's house; you shall not covet your neighbor's wife, nor his male servant, nor his female servant, nor his ox, nor his donkey, nor anything that is your neighbor's."* (NKJV)

It seems pretty straightforward yet Catholics, Jews and Protestants divide these 14 verses up differently to create a different set of Ten Commandments. I could list the arguments for how these commandments should be divided, but the fact is, it doesn't really matter what we "name" as the specific "ten". It is all the Word of God. It is His list of commandments and there are actually more than ten commands given. So, in spite of the varying beliefs recognized by the three religious groups, God still gave all of the mandates. I believe we should be more concerned with obeying all of the verses and not be overly concerned with their division.

That being said, we can now address the question at hand. Is it okay to pray before a statue? If we look at verse 4 we can see that there is a clear mandate against the carving of images that represent anyone or anything in heaven, or even on earth. Does this mean that God is opposed to artistic representations of people or heavenly beings? Hardly!

As we study, we need to read the context of the verses. So let's look at the layout of this "list of instructions". In the first half of the "list" God is citing the decrees that directly affect our relationship to Him. In the second half, the commands involve our relationship to each other.

When we read *"You shall have no other gods before me"* it is clear that God wants to be "exclusive" in our lives. But He goes further, *"You shall not make for yourself a carved image"*, *"You shall not take the name of the LORD your God in vain"* and *"Remember the Sabbath day, to keep it holy."* All of these verses show us how God is jealous for our devotion. He wants our worship, complete and undividedly.

So why would He prohibit carved images? Some would argue that He meant images like the idols of that day, used by the peoples around them as gods. But the verse says specifically that the forbidden images are of *"any likeness of anything that is in heaven above"* which includes God Himself. So the commandment is saying that you're not allowed to make any image that represents any being regardless of its status. In other words, we can't claim that making a statue of Buddha is wrong, but a statue of Jesus is okay. God does not want our relationship to Him to look like the pagan worship around the world.

The purpose in having statues is to aid the Catholic in his or her prayers. In debating this issue, a Catholic said that because God commanded the making of statues in the Bible, it cannot be wrong for us to do the same. He quotes the verses in Exodus 25 *"You shall make two cherubim of gold;..... The cherubim shall spread out their wings above, overshadowing the mercy seat with their wings..."* (NRSV) God's instructions for the Ark of the Covenant included the creating of these two angels of gold. Another instance he mentions in Scripture is found in Numbers 21 where a plague of serpents had come upon the Israelites as punishment and God instructs Moses to make a serpent of bronze to hold up on a pole. When the people looked at the bronze "statue" they were healed of their snakebite.

So if God instructs the making and use of statues, what's wrong with the Catholic use of statues? If we use the above verses in Exodus and Numbers to defend the making of statues, we need to look at them more closely.

First, God's instructions to make the gold cherubim for the Ark of the Covenant are merely for artistic beauty. At **no** time do the priests bow to these angels or pray to them. In fact the temple of Solomon included carved angels along the inner walls, covered in gold. Yet, they were **only** there for decoration. No one ever knelt before them to pray to who they represented.

Secondly, the bronze serpent that Moses made to heal the Israelites from the plague of serpents was specifically done as a foreshadowing of Christ. Many times throughout Old Testament Scripture are signs of the coming Messiah. They are forms of prophecy which prove Who Jesus is. In John 3:14 Jesus says *"And just as Moses lifted up the serpent in the wilderness, so must the Son of Man be lifted up, that whoever believes in him may have eternal life."* (NRSV) The Catholic defender argued "One had to look at the bronze statue of the serpent to be healed, which shows that statues could be used ritually, not merely as religious decorations." Though it is true that God used this image to heal His people, it was **not** prayed to, only looked at. And furthermore, the end result of having this bronze serpent led the people of Israel into idol worship. In 2nd Kings 18 we are told that Hezekiah broke the bronze serpent into pieces because the people were burning incense to it.

After pointing out these arguments from Scripture, this Catholic advocate claims "it's not wrong for us to use images of these forms to deepen our knowledge and love of God." My question here is why does it take a statue to "deepen our knowledge and love of God"?

God knows our human tendency to idolize things. He tells us not to create graven images because as humans we can easily be misled. History is filled with incidents of idolatry because of "harmless" images. We see even today how much emphasis is put on the images instead of Jesus. I can attest to this myself in an incident that took place not too long ago near my home.

A hospital nearby had a window that developed condensation between the panes of glass. The moisture formed an "image" of what looked like the Madonna. This display drew a lot of attention and within days there was a crowd of onlookers, mostly Catholics, coming to get a glimpse of what they reported to be a miracle. The numerous responses to this included what people called an "appearance of the Blessed Mother".

There were people praying, asking Mary for healing, help or peace. One mother said "I bring my kids here — hopefully it will bring some inner peace to them and to me." Many others stood saying the rosary, some with tears in their eyes, all because of an "image" appearing in a window. And whether or not it really looked like Mary holding baby Jesus didn't matter. People saw what they wanted to see.

The point of sharing this story is to shed light on why God doesn't want us to make "images" for the purpose of worship or prayer. Satan can, and will use whatever means to distract us from our devotion to God. Just like the "miraculous" occasions where statues have been seen crying or bleeding. These occurrences only draw attention to themselves and cause people to be more interested in the miracle rather than God.

Satan has the ability to perform wonders and when

we get caught up in the miraculous signs we lose our focus. That is why Jesus said in Matthew 12:39 *"An evil and adulterous generation asks for a sign*(miracle)*"* (NRSV) Our attention to God is diminished when we allow ourselves to use images as tools of adoration.

As we learned from the first commandments, God wants our sole devotion. When we incorporate images to "assist" us in worship, our focus on Christ is blurred. We no longer look to Him directly, but want something tangible and visible. And what about our faith? Hebrews 11:1 says *"Now faith is the assurance of things hoped for, the conviction of things not seen."* (NRSV) If we have true faith in God we won't need to see Him to pray to Him. In fact, statues only show a lack of faith in the believer to trust in an unseen God.

# – 7 –

# Purgatory

"We must pray for the souls in purgatory", Sister said. "With our prayers, they will soon enter heaven."

According to the Catholic catechism, purgatory is "A condition of suffering after death, in which souls make up for their sins before they enter heaven."

This doctrine was introduced in 593 A.D., and proclaimed a dogma in 1493 A.D. It was established by Pope Gregory I, and has no Biblical basis, nor does apostolic tradition speak of it. It took 593 years before the idea was even suggested, and still another almost 850 years after that, before it became dogma, meaning it was to be taught as absolute truth.

In his book "Roman Catholicism", H.B. Coxon writes, concerning the doctrine of purgatory, "But let the more difficult and subtle questions, both those which tend not to edification and those from which, for the most part, there is no increase of piety, be excluded from popular discourses before the uneducated multitude."

In brief, what he is saying is that any questions that

arise that do not agree with this doctrine, should be dismissed and not brought before the lay people in the church, which he calls "the uneducated multitude."

This statement makes two mistakes. First it presumes that such a doctrine is correct, but makes no allowance for proving it so. Then it refuses to educate the congregation on the facts and thus, keeps the people ignorant. This is how such fallacies become dogma in the first place. The congregation was not allowed to question such things.

We read in Hebrews 10:14, *"For by a single offering he has perfected for all time those who are sanctified."* (NRSV) This verse of Scripture maintains the same truth that has been discussed in previous chapters - Jesus died once, to take away all of our sin. The Bible is very specific to mention that with one offering, we are made forever perfect. Not only does Christ not have to suffer anymore, but neither do we, because we are made perfect.

Even in the light of this certainty, Catholic teaching still assumes that Christ continues to suffer in the Eucharist, and in addition to that, we are still obligated to pay for our sins with penance and in purgatory.

The Bible does talk about our "life" after death. To know for sure just what will happen to us when we die, we must depend on God's Word. Hebrews 9:27 states, *"And just as it is appointed for mortals to die once, and after that the judgment,"* (NRSV) there is no mention of purgatory found in the Bible; not even anything like it.

Throughout Scripture, we read over and over of how the sacrifice of our Lord paid in full the penalty of all sin. The only account of suffering after death is in reference to hell, and to those who will be cast into it.

When approached with this assurance a devout Catholic argued one point. "It is not fair," she objected, "What about those who sin worse than others?" With this attitude a person sets a "standard" by which some sinners are worse than others. In other words, we have rated sin in degrees of bad to very bad, etc.

This is not God's view of sin. He is an all perfect and righteous God and cannot have sin in His presence. Not even the least of sinners can enter heaven. That's why Jesus' sinless body made the perfect sacrifice. By this sacrifice God sees only a righteous person, pure and sinless.

If we claim that we deserve to go to heaven more so, because we are not as bad as someone else, then we are alleging that heaven is something we have to work for. Scripture holds to just the opposite of this. It says that salvation is a "free gift".

But let us go even further. In the Catholic Church sin is separated into two degrees, mortal and venial. According to the Catechism, a mortal sin is a "very bad" sin and "deprives the sinner of sanctifying grace". A person who commits a mortal sin can still avoid hell if, as stated by the Church, he goes to confession and repents of such sin. However, he still must pay the penalty in purgatory.

Let us look at a well known passage of Scripture. Recorded in the Gospel of Luke 23:33-43 are the events that took place during Christ's crucifixion. We read that two criminals hung beside Jesus. One of the criminals insulted Jesus but the other criminal defended Him. Verse 42 tells us that *"Then he said, "Jesus, remember me when you come into your kingdom."* (NRSV) and Jesus replied *"Truly I tell you, today you will be with me in Paradise."* (NRSV) There is no question that this man was a sinner. It is also obvious that he had committed a serious crime since he was receiving the death penalty. According to Catholic teaching, he would certainly have spent time in purgatory; however, Jesus said today you will be in paradise. No purgatory here!

Biblical teaching goes against the idea of purgatory. The whole purpose of Christ's death was to eliminate completely the punishment for sin.

Let us look at what the apostle Paul wrote about the forgiveness of sins, keeping in mind that Paul was a man responsible for the death and persecution of many Christians before he became one himself. Paul's statement, as recorded in Acts 13:38-39 is, *"Through this man forgiveness of sins is proclaimed to you; by this Jesus everyone who believes is set free from all those sins."* (NRSV) Paul is telling us that no matter what we have done, we can be freed from the penalty of our sin, if we trust in Jesus. He says we will be made righteous. That does not mean that we will not continue to sin. Just as discussed in Chapter 5, temptation is still a part of our earthly lives. That is why God sent us the Holy Spirit; to help us stand against temptation.

In regard to our disobedience though, we can depend on the single sacrifice of Christ to cleanse us, not only from our past sins, but also the sins we have not yet committed.

Again, the Catholic Church indicates with the doctrine of purgatory, the need to make up for sin. This is demonstrated best by the role of "indulgences". According to the Catechism, "An indulgence is the removal of some or all of the temporal punishment for sin that we should have had to suffer on earth or in purgatory." Indulgences are granted by the Church to the Catholic who fulfills a certain act. This reward is supposed to help the sinner earn his way into heaven, without having to spend much, if any, time in purgatory.

Romans 3:21-24 states, *"But now God has shown us a different way to heaven—not by "being good enough" and trying to keep his laws, but by a new way (though not new, really, for the Scriptures told about it long ago). Now God says he will accept and acquit us—declare us "not guilty"—if we trust Jesus Christ to take away our sins. And we all can be saved in this same way, by coming to Christ, no matter who we are or what we have been like. Yes, all have sinned; all fall short of God's glorious ideal; yet now God declares us "not guilty" of offending him if we trust in Jesus Christ, who in his kindness freely takes away our sins."* (TLB)

But to continue, Romans 3:26, states, *"But isn't this*

*unfair for God to let criminals go free and say they are innocent? No, for He does it on the basis of their trust in Jesus, who took away their sins."* (TLB) The very issue we are discussing was settled here in the book of Romans. Continuing with verses 27-28, *"Our acquittal is not based on our good deeds; it is based on what Christ has done and our faith in Him. So it is that we are justified by faith and not by the good things we do."* (TLB)

This is the most distinct passage of Scripture explaining our justification. It could not be more clearly stated that we <u>cannot</u> earn our way into heaven. All the good deeds in the world <u>cannot</u> make you righteous enough for God's kingdom.

This reference from Ephesians 2:8-9 explains further, *"For by grace you have been saved through faith, and this is not your own doing; it is the gift of God—not the result of works, so that no one may boast."* (NRSV)

The only way we can enter heaven is through our faith in Christ. And this salvation is totally free. It did not cost us anything! Because it is free, no one will be able to boast and no one will enter heaven saying "I got here because I was so good." No matter how good you are, you are not good enough for heaven. Faith in Christ is the only way heaven can be available to you.

Now, if we look clearly at all that we have discussed, it is quite evident that we neither earn our way to heaven with our works, nor do we pay for our sins in purgatory after we die. If we receive salvation by our faith in Christ, then heaven is a certainty. This salvation does not mean we will stop sinning, but the issue of sin after we're saved, is brought to light in the book of Romans 3:31, *"Well then, if we are saved by faith, does this mean that we no longer need to obey God's laws? Just the opposite! In fact, only when we trust Jesus can we truly obey Him."* (TLB)

Accepting Jesus and trusting in Him will bring you salvation - not by good deeds, but by faith alone. It is through this faith that we can lead a righteous life and please God. In fact, true obedience to God will only come when we are saved, because only then will we have the power of the Holy Spirit inside us to keep us from living a sinful life.

# – 8 –

# Justification

Justification is not so difficult to understand as some believe it is. Quite simply it means "to be justified" or "to be made right". It is used in religion to explain how a person can be made right with God and enter heaven. For example, in the previous chapter we looked at purgatory and how, according to Catholic teaching, a person is not justified until his soul is purged through the punishment of purgatory. The Bible teaches that justification comes with our faith in Christ. We read in Romans 3:28, *"For we hold that a person is justified by faith apart from works prescribed by the law."* (NRSV)

Although this justification through faith alone is clearly taught in the Bible, Catholicism continues to add the need for "good works" to complete the justification.

The scripture verse below is often quoted by Catholic theologians to support the doctrine of "faith + works = salvation". Unfortunately, it is again blatantly misinterpreted. James 2:24, states, *"You see that a person is justified by works and not by faith alone."* (NRSV)

If this was the only verse in the Bible on justification, there would be no need to argue with the Catholic view of being justified. However, if we compare this reference from James, with the passages we mentioned in Romans 3, and numerous others, including Ephesians 2:8-9, which states, *"For by grace you have been saved through faith, and this is not your own doing; it is the gift of God—not the result of works, so that no one may boast."* (NRSV) there is a definite contrast of meanings.

The Bible is God's true Word and cannot contradict itself and Catholicism would agree with this truth. So how can these two verses shown above be so conflicting? The fact is that they do not contradict at all. The verse in James must be understood in the context of the whole book. For instance, the 2nd chapter of James, talks about those who <u>claim</u> to have faith. Verse 14 states, *What good is it, my brothers and sisters, if you say you have faith but do not have works? Can faith save you?"* (NRSV) James is questioning the man whose faith does not seem legitimate because his actions do not "justify" him. James continues this discussion about the need to demonstrate ones faith by the good works one does.

So when we look at verse 24, above, we can see that James is talking about a man who is justified by his works. However, he is not justified to **God**, but to <u>man</u>. The man's works justify him before others and prove that he really is saved.

The book of James is not dealing with the doctrine

of salvation, but the relationship between Christians. When we attempt to identify someone as a Christian, we can look at their deeds to see if they are "justified" in our eyes as a true follower of Christ. A very good example of this type of justification is summed up by Peter in 1 Peter 2:12, *"Conduct yourselves honorably among the Gentiles, so that, though they malign you as evildoers, they may see your honorable deeds and glorify God when he comes to judge."* (NRSV)

When we are true followers of Christ our lives should be different from those who are of the world. James warned the early Christians that they should beware of those who "claim" to be Christians, and he gave the signs for judging such a claim. Good deeds don't bring you salvation, but they indicate that you are indeed saved.

# – 9 –

# The Papacy

"And the Pope is the closest one to God", the C.C.D. teacher's words still echoed in my mind. I thought to myself, "she can't be serious." Yet she was indeed sincere, as she taught the group of 6th and 7th graders.

I was sitting in on this class that my younger sister was attending. I felt a great desire to counter what this woman was teaching her students, however, I remained silent.

Who is the Pope? The Catechism teaches that he is "the vicar of Christ" and the "chief teacher and leader of God's people." This is a brief definition stating that the Pope is basically the "boss" in the Catholic Church.

The authority given to the Pope includes a tremendous amount of power in regard to the Catholic Church. He is considered, among other things, as the one who "holds the place of Jesus in the Church". This is why the C.C.D. teacher felt so sincerely that the Pope was the closest one to God.

To support this teaching, the Catholic Church

quotes Matthew 16:18, which states, *"And I tell you, you are Peter, and on this rock I will build my church, and the gates of Hades will not prevail against it."* (NRSV) According to Catholic belief, Christ here names Peter head of His church, by claiming that Peter is the one rock on which Christ intends the church to be built.

First of all, we must take a closer look at the words that Christ used. As we know, the original language of the New Testament was Greek, and we are reading the translated version in English. Christ said *"you are Peter"*. Here, Peter is the Greek word "petros", which actually means a piece of rock or stone. In contrast, Christ says He will build His church on *"this rock"*. Here the Greek word "petra" is used, which means a mass of rock or large rock.

Christ deliberately used separate terms to assure His point. He did not say, "You are Peter and on <u>you</u> I will build my church". The words have different meanings which give the whole statement a different view.

What then did Christ really mean? Well, if we look at the whole context of Matthew 16, we can more easily understand Christ's intent. In the verses preceding verse 18, it is written that Jesus is with His disciples and He asks them who they think He is. Peter answers by saying that Jesus is the Son of God. That is when Christ says in verse 17, " *"Blessed are you, Simon son of Jonah! For flesh and blood has not revealed this to you, but my Father in heaven."* (NRSV) He continues in verse 18 with, *"And I tell you, you are Peter, and on this rock I will build my church, and the gates of Hades will not prevail against it."* (NRSV)

If we look at it in this setting, it makes more sense that Jesus was using Peter's *answer* to explain the foundation of the Church. The Rock that Christ intends His church to be built on is Himself. He is affirming Peter's response that He is the Messiah, Peter is the stone, and Christ is the Rock.

Catholicism teaches that Christ was giving Peter a special job to be head of the whole church. This theory is not consistent with Scripture. Peter is used to build the Church of Christ, but he is not the primary leader. In Ephesians 2:20, Paul tells the church in Ephesus, *"you are . . . built upon the foundation of the apostles and prophets, with Christ Jesus himself as the cornerstone."* (NRSV) Therefore, Peter is not the foundation of the church; he is only a part of the foundation.

If anyone knew what Christ was talking about, it would have been Peter himself. After all, Christ was talking to him. Consequently, let us see what Peter has to say about this. In 1 Peter 2:4, he states, *"Come to Christ who is the living foundation of rock upon which God builds."* (TLB) Christ is the true foundation. Verse 5 continues, *"and now you have become living building stones for God's use in building His house."* (TLB) Here, Peter is admitting that we all make up the church as stones, and that Christ is the chief cornerstone.

Certainly, Peter would have claimed some more significant part in this foundation if Christ had, indeed, given him such authority. Apparently, he did not conclude the same belief that Catholics teach. He understood Jesus' statement perfectly. Christ the Rock — Peter one stone among many.

Another passage of Scripture applied to the Papacy is found in John 21:15-17, Jesus asks Peter, *"Simon son of John, do you love me more than these?"* (NRSV) Peter answers, *"Yes Lord."* Jesus responds, *"Feed my lambs".* Jesus asks Peter again if he loves Him, and Peter again replies, *"Yes Lord".* Jesus repeats *"Tend my sheep".* For the third time Jesus asks Peter about his love for Him. At this point Peter is hurt, but says *"yes"* and Christ reiterates *"Feed my sheep".*

According to Catholic belief, Christ was giving Peter the exclusive privilege of shepherding His flock. In the verse mentioned above, however, Jesus was reinstating Peter as His servant. Just days before, Peter had denied Christ three times (John 18:17,25 & 27). Jesus questioned Peter's love for Him that it might be reinforced. He gave Peter a fresh start and delegated a position to him in His church.

The responsibility Christ appointed Peter was that of a shepherd to a flock. The flock, however, was not intended to represent the entire church, and the shepherd was not intended to rule over it. Peter was simply being asked to take part in the overall ministry of Christ. He even tells us in his own book 1 Peter 5:2-3, *"Shepherd the flock of God which is among you, serving as overseers,. . . not as being lords over those entrusted to you, but being examples to the flock."* (NKJV) Peter defines the purpose of the shepherd not to be a ruler, but a teacher and example. This also indicates that there are many shepherds, not just Peter.

We read in Acts 20:28, *"Keep watch over yourselves and over all the flock, of which the Holy Spirit has made you overseers, to shepherd the church of God that he obtained with the blood of his own Son"* (NRSV) Again, this confirms the existence of many shepherds.

The best way to substantiate the role of Peter would be to look at his life after Jesus ascended to Heaven. The overall history of the first church is recorded in the book of Acts. The book begins with Jesus' ascension, the replacement of Judas with Matthias as the twelfth apostle, and Pentecost. After receiving the Holy Spirit at Pentecost, the apostles go out and preach the Gospel.

Here, at the beginning of the Christian ministry, Peter is mentioned as one who first addresses the crowds. He is also the first one recorded as performing a miracle, with John at the temple, when he healed a crippled man. The chapter continues with Peter and John's arrest, and their dealings with the Jewish leaders. Chapter five mentions Peter again in a leadership role, as he talks with some new believers about greed.

Peter is shown here, in the beginning of Acts, as a leader and a "shepherd". He is mentioned many times in these first few chapters and comes across as a very important person in the development of Christ's church. Obviously, Peter's role in the early church is significant, but that does not mean he was the single leader of the church.

Peter is in no way referred to by the other apostles as the authority figure. In Acts 8, Philip has converted many people in Samaria with preaching and healing. Verse 14 of the same chapter proceeds, *"Now when the apostles at Jerusalem heard that Samaria had accepted the word of God, they sent Peter and John to them."* (NRSV) Peter was sent to Samaria – he did not make the decision to go there on his own. This is just one instance of Peter's lack of authority in the dealings of the new church.

In Acts 15:6, a discussion among the apostles and elders began concerning the conversion of the Gentiles. This major issue was addressed at this meeting by Peter, Paul and Barnabas. Yet it was not until James spoke up and reaffirmed what had already been said that a final decision was made. Certainly if Peter was at all an authority figure over these men, there would have been no argument. Peter was not in control at this or any other meeting among the apostles or elders of the church. In fact, after this crucial decision was made, the ones appointed to go and spread the news were Paul, Barnabas, Jude and Silas.

Peter did not play a major role in the outcome of the first significant doctrinal ruling. If he was the first "Pope", as the Catholic Church teaches, he unquestionably does not demonstrate it. Also, in comparison to Peter, Paul is an even more significant apostle in the Bible. It was

Paul who wrote 100 chapters consisting of 2,325 verses of Scripture. Peter wrote only 8 chapters of 166 verses. Paul played an outstanding role in the early church. He was the primary *"apostle to the Gentiles"*, as stated in Galatians 2:11. Peter on the other hand, ministered primarily to Jews. This undoubtedly differs from the role of the Catholic Pope.

Paul even writes of himself in 2 Corinthians 11:5, *"I think that I am not in the least inferior to these super-apostles."* (NRSV) If Peter had been given authority over the church, Paul would certainly have not made such a statement. After all, he would have to consider himself even a little inferior to Peter, if Peter was indeed in charge of him.

Paul goes even further than to regard himself equal with Peter by actually rebuking him. We read in Galatians 2:11, Paul's statement, *"Now when Peter had come to Antioch, I withstood him to his face, because he was to be blamed."* (NKJV) Paul is referring to an incident where Peter had been eating with the Gentiles. However, some of the other apostles showed up and Peter immediately separated himself from the Gentiles. He acted like a hypocrite.

Paul even mentions how Peter's prejudice caused others to sin. In Galatians 2:13, he continues, *"And the other Jews joined him in this hypocrisy, so that even Barnabas was led astray by their hypocrisy."* (NRSV) Here, Peter is not only in the wrong, but he is leading others into sin as well.

**Paul** straightened out this situation. Peter has no authority over Paul and, in fact, was subordinate to Paul in this case. How then can we consider Peter a Pope? If indeed Peter was the first Pope, he would not have been rebuked by Paul and he would have taken charge of the issue of dealing with the Gentiles. Yet, after this incident, Peter speaks highly of Paul. 2nd Peter 3:15-16, Peter states, *"So also our beloved brother Paul wrote to you according to the wisdom given him,… There are some things in them hard to understand, which the ignorant and unstable twist to their own destruction, as they do the other scriptures."* (NRSV) Here Peter affirms Paul's writings as Scripture.

Another instance of Paul's position in the early church is found in Act 24:5 where Paul is on trial and the Jewish attorney brings this charge against him; *"We have, in fact, found this man a pestilent fellow, an agitator among all the Jews throughout the world, and a ringleader of the sect of the Nazarenes"* (NRSV) Here, **Paul** is called the "ringleader" of the Christian movement. The Greek word used here is "prōtostatēs" which means "one standing first in the ranks, that is, a captain" This certainly contradicts the "leadership" role of Peter in the church.

Another Catholic claim of Peter's position is that he is said to be the first bishop of Rome. This is because Rome is where the first Pope originated. The book of Romans, is Paul's letter to Rome. It was written at the time when Peter is said to have been in Rome acting as "bishop" of that church. Paul closes out this letter to Rome, having greeted many people; but there is no mention of Peter at all. Paul does not send greetings to Peter? There can be no other conclusion than to believe that Peter was not there. If he had been there, Paul would have, without a doubt, said hello to him.

There is no scriptural or historical evidence that even suggests that Peter was stationed in Rome. Throughout his ministry, Peter remained in the East. How then can it be claimed that Peter was the first bishop of Rome, when it cannot even be verified that he was ever there? Roman Catholic theology teaches that Peter was given a special authority over Christ's Church. There is no indication at all in Scripture that this is true and, in fact, it goes against Scripture.

Historically, the church did not even have a Pope until 590 A.D. Before this time the Roman bishop was in charge only of the Church in Rome. Almost 600 years after the start of the church, the first Pope, Gregory I, was only in authority over those dioceses that agreed to submit to him. It was not until 1054 that a split came between the Eastern and Western churches. The Eastern Church did not want to submit to a Pope. It was at this time that the Roman Catholic Church first gave the Pope total authority over its Western church. Yet, even the first Pope was very different from the Pope of today. He was not considered infallible like the present Pope. The doctrine of infallibility was not established until 1870.

According to the Catholic Catechism, the duties of the Pope include "teaching, governing and guiding Catholics in what they believe and in how they live." This role in the church is to some degree what Christ intended for those chosen to be the "shepherds" or ministers. Christ did not, however, designate a single man to be in charge of the entire church.

The role which is assumed by the Pope possesses a great amount of power. He is looked upon as the man closest to God. He is alleged to have a special gift of infallibility "when teaching a truth of faith or right living." This ability to be free from mistakes when teaching about faith is said to come from the Holy Spirit. According to the Catechism, it is important to follow the Pope because "the Holy Spirit guides him in teaching us what to believe and do in order to be saved." It is believed that the Holy Spirit guides the Pope in the teaching of the church. Therefore, if the Pope is speaking on the subject of faith and morals, and is "directed" by the Holy Spirit, then his statements regarding such are proclaimed "excathedra". This means they are infallible.

The Holy Spirit is our main source of guidance. It is through this third person of the Trinity that we are given direction. Jesus told his disciples that He would send a Helper. This Helper was the Holy Spirit. At Pentecost, the Holy Spirit came to the twelve apostles. Peter was not the only one to receive the Holy Spirit. In fact, after his experience, Peter talks to a crowd of unbelievers and says, *"Repent, and be baptized every one of you … and you will receive the gift of the Holy Spirit"* (NRSV) (Acts 2:38). So it is, that all believers will receive the Holy Spirit when they turn to Christ.

The fact that each believer has the Holy Spirit shows the inadequacy of this role of the Pope. The Holy Spirit cannot make a mistake because He is God. The Pope, however, is merely a man, and although he can be directed by the Holy Spirit, he can also be influenced by Satan. To say that any man is completely free from the tempting of the devil is totally wrong. Satan is sly and deceptive, and he would do anything to mislead people away from God. There is no place in the Bible that affirms the doctrine of infallibility. If we accept the doctrines of the Pope as infallibly from God, then we are putting our faith and trust in a man. Satan is still the master of deceit and no one, not even the Pope, is free from error!

The Pope is called "Holy Father", a name that is exclusively given to God the Father in the Bible. In the eye of the public (Catholic community), the Pope is considered to be above everyone. While greeting his "flock", many of those near him strive to touch his robe or kiss his ring, much like those who met Christ; yet Christ was God. In all of this, the Pope makes no attempt to equate himself with these followers. Typically, we can picture the Pope holding a hand up in a manner to bless those who bow before him.

Peter, in comparison, demonstrates his position perfectly in Acts 10:24-26, which tells of how Peter goes to visit Cornelius, a Roman officer. *"On Peter's arrival Cornelius met him, and falling at his feet, worshiped him. But Peter made him get up, saying, "Stand up; I am only a mortal."* (NRSV) Does this sound like the Pope? Does the Peter in the Bible coincide with the image of today's Pope? Hardly!

The Bible is very clear as to what sort of authority was truly handed down by Christ. The establishment of the Papacy was not Christ ordained. It was instituted by men, and therefore, cannot be considered valid by God. Jesus is the head of the church. Trusting in a man as a faultless leader puts us in a dangerous position and exposes us to the wiles of the devil. Satan can and does use his power to deceive and manipulate, and Jesus Christ is the only One Who is stronger than him.

# – 10 –
# The Worship of Mary

"When you want something, you always go to your mother first. She can ask your father for you. She has special favor with him." This is the response I received when I asked the question, "Why do you pray to Mary?" This reply is very commonly given by most Catholics who are asked the same question.

To worship something or someone other than God is idolatry. The Catholic Church considers this a very grave sin This definition from the Catechism is quite accurate; "Idolatry is giving to a creature, the supreme honor due to God alone." By their own admission the worship of Mary would be a terrible offense.

I believe that the Catholic Church promotes the worship of Mary. The church, however, claims that they do not worship her, but rather honor her. I trust that through the following paragraphs, it will become evident how much the church really does worship the one they call the "Blessed Virgin".

To begin, we must first convey exactly what the

church maintains as their position on the worship of Mary. Their stand on this point is the same as it has been for many years. It is best explained in the Catechism. "Worship belongs only to God whom we shall adore. Adoration is the worship we give to God alone, as the infinitely Holy and Supreme Being. Veneration is the honor we give to the Blessed Virgin as the Mother of God." This is their reasoning: Worship? No. Honor and venerate? Yes.

Now, let us discuss the terms, honor, venerate and worship. Honor: "to treat with respect, revere". Venerate: "to hold in highest respect, revere." Worship: "to perform religious service; to reverence, adore." All of these definitions are taken from the same Webster's Dictionary. All three definitions indicate the word reverence or revere.

We can say that to honor God or to worship God is the same thing. To show honor to someone does not indicate idolatry, but when we use the word worship, it goes beyond just honoring. Worship is giving full devotion to someone and placing them not just above ourselves, but everyone. We worship God because we believe He is the Supreme Being.

Honoring Mary as the earthly mother of Jesus is certainly appropriate. The same honor is due for all those who served with Jesus faithfully. Honor and worship are two words with a fine line between meanings. Yet, by reviewing Catholic tradition and teaching, it is apparent that it is more than honor that is given to Mary. In fact, the church has consistently tried to elevate Mary to a place equal with Christ. This is not only idolatry, but apostasy as well.

I know these are strong words, but please understand that we are dealing with God, the One and only true God and as the Bible states in Exodus 34:14; *"you shall worship no other god, because the Lord, whose name is Jealous, is a jealous God."* (NRSV) God shares His place with <u>no one</u>. Catholic teaching, however, has over many centuries, equated Mary with Christ and acclaimed her to deity. Of course the Catholic Church will continually deny this, but following are the steps to deity which the church has taken to, as they say, "honor" Mary.

Although the church denies teaching that Mary is a goddess, it continues to exalt Mary and encourages worship to her. The Bible contains eighteen references to Jesus' mother. These Scripture passages will be used throughout this chapter to help us understand the truth about Mary and her place in the Christian's life.

**Step one:** Mary the Mother of God. This is the title often used when referring to Jesus' mother. Catholic's explain "Mary is really the Mother of God, because she is the Mother of Jesus who is God." At first glance, this sounds rational, but we must look deeper into this concept.

Mary is the mother of Jesus. Jesus is God, but He is only one part of the Trinity. He is God the Son. As God the Son, Jesus took on flesh and became a man. This made Him a God-man. He was not just man and not just God. Mary was the mother of the flesh of Jesus. She gave birth to the man of Jesus, not to His Deity.

God as the one true God has always existed. Jesus has always existed with God the Father and even refers to His physical body as being separate from His deity in this passage from Hebrews 10:5, ". . . *but a body you prepared for me.*" Jesus existed long before Mary ever did. Jesus even makes reference to His Deity and His existence before man in the book of John 8:58, *"Jesus said to them, "Very truly, I tell you, before Abraham was, I am."* (NRSV) Jesus is God in the fullest sense, and so He used the term "I am" because that expressed the eternity of His being and His oneness with the Father.

Mary did not mother the Trinity, nor did she give birth to the deity of Jesus. She cannot, therefore, be the mother of God. Calling Mary the "Mother of God" only serves to equate her with Jesus being the "Son of God".

**Step two:** the "Immaculate Conception". This feast celebrated by the Catholic Church refers to the conception of Mary. In 1854, Pope Pius 9th, declared Mary "to be free from the stain of original sin". The Catechism states that Mary "in view of the merits of her divine Son, was preserved from original sin from the moment of her conception." The church goes on to claim that Mary remained totally sinless throughout her life.

There is no reference at all made to Mary's birth in the Bible in regard to this claim. Scripture states plainly in Romans 3:23, *"all have sinned and fall short of the glory of God."* (NRSV) To affirm this truth, we read in Romans 5:12, *"and so death spread to all because all have sinned."* (NRSV) We can analyze this up and down, but no matter how we look at it, the truth is, we all are guilty of sin. Mary was no different and falls into the same category we do. She was a sinner like us.

The Bible describes Mary as a submissive and faithful girl. We are told that God found favor with her. Obviously, Mary was a virtuous woman who must have had a good up-bringing. God recognized her as being honorable and felt she would be suitable for His purpose.

In spite of her righteousness, however, it cannot be assumed that she was free from sin. To make such a claim, we must be able to support it with Scripture. Yet the Bible contradicts such teaching. In addition to the Bible verses given above, let us look deeper into the God's Word.

We are told that *"all have sinned"* but if that is not proof enough, let us see what Mary has to say about herself. In the first chapter of Luke, the angel Gabriel announces to Mary the coming of the Christ. She is told that she will bear the Son of God. Mary was brought up in the Jewish faith and she knows about the prophecies regarding the Messiah. She is aware that this Messiah is being sent by God to save His people from their sin.

In Luke 1:46-55, Mary recites a prayer of thanksgiving to God. She begins by saying in verse 47, *"My soul magnifies the Lord, and my spirit rejoices in God my Savior."* (NRSV) Mary calls God her Savior. Only a sinner needs a savior, and Mary knew that even she was not sinless. Throughout Scripture, no one except Jesus Christ is called Holy. He <u>alone</u> was born without sin. Mary's so-called "Immaculate Conception" is a fabrication from the minds of men.

In my quest to find the origin of this Catholic teaching, I corresponded with a priest on the matter of the "Immaculate Conception". I really wanted to know just how this claim could possibly be explained logically. His reply stated this: "Mary needed to be redeemed, so quotes(from the Bible) that seem to contradict the Immaculate Conception need to be read in the light of the meaning of that doctrine, i.e., that Mary <u>was</u> redeemed, but in an altogether <u>special way</u>." Here is a priest's meager attempt to justify this doctrine.

Let us just <u>suppose</u> this explanation is right. God decides to single out Mary and redeem her in this "special way" so that she can bring Jesus into the world without having sin within herself. Two very big questions would have to be raised. One is, how could Mary's mother produce Mary if she had sin in her life? Was Mary's mother sinless too? And her grandmother, and so on? Undoubtedly not. And second, if God had another way of redeeming, why then did He send His Son to die? Someone once said, if God had another way to save us, then He is essentially guilty of "child abuse" because that would mean He sent His son to suffer and die needlessly.

If Mary was, in fact, sinless by this special act of God,

then the whole plan of salvation would be completely different from the Biblical design God intended. The Bible, in no manner, follows along with this theory that Mary was free from sin.

To further the church's attempt to explain this doctrine, I read a passage from a book that teaches Catholic doctrine, <u>The Doctrines of God the Redeemer</u>. In the chapter regarding the "Immaculate Conception", these quotes were found: "The doctrine of the Immaculate Conception of Mary <u>is not explicitly revealed in Scripture</u>." They continue that it is "implied" in this passage of Genesis 3:15, *"I will put enmity between you and the woman, and between your offspring and hers; he* (seed of the woman) *will strike your head, and you will strike his heel."* (NRSV) This passage is considered to be the first prophecy regarding the Messiah. The serpent whom God is talking to is Satan, and God is foretelling of the future war between Satan and his followers, and Eve and her descendants. The seed that crushes Satan's head is called <u>he</u> and directly refers to Christ.

The book continues, using the passage from Genesis and explains, "The seed of the woman was understood as referring to the Redeemer and, thus, the <u>Mother</u> of the Redeemer <u>came to be seen</u> in the woman." Here they attempt to include Mary in this Messianic prophecy by saying that she "came to be seen" in the woman. They continue, "According to this interpretation, Mary stands <u>with</u> Christ in a perfect and victorious enmity towards Satan." This is disgraceful! They falsely incorporate

Mary in this passage that directly refers to Christ. God is addressing Satan with Eve and the seed of Eve is referred to as he, Jesus Christ. How can we honestly believe that Jesus' mother is included in that verse. Other than the fact that she gave birth to His humanity, she had no role in the process of the redemption which required His Deity.

To complicate things even more, this theory leads to another assumption. The book goes on to say that if Mary did stand with Christ in a victory over Satan then "consequently she must have entered this world without the stain of original sin." They just get in deeper and deeper. One assumption leads to another and that is how this doctrine was instituted in the first place.

To sum it all up, the book makes one last attempt to rationalize this dogma. "Thus, it is fitting that Christ should redeem His mother", referring to a "pre-redemption" that Mary received at the moment she was conceived. Their final argument to support such a doctrine ends like this: "(God could do it, He ought to do it, therefore, He did it). This, it is true, gives no certainty, but still, it rationally establishes for the dogma a high degree of probability."

This is a direct quote from the book mentioned. There could not be a more futile attempt at rationalization than this. It is true that God can do all things, but no one has the right to say God ought to do anything. By making that statement, they are acting as God and that is wrong. Yet the church says God ought to have done it, and so He did? No. God shows us the truth in His Word, and it is not "implied" it is very explicit.

First John 1:8, states, *"If we say that we have no sin, we deceive ourselves, and the truth is not in us."* (NRSV) This could also suggest claiming someone else to be without sin. To make the point even more obvious, we must look at a very important part in Scripture concerning this. We read in Luke 2:22&24, *"When the time came for their purification according to the law of Moses, they brought him up to Jerusalem to present him to the Lord. . . and they offered a sacrifice according to what is stated in the law of the Lord, "a pair of turtledoves or two young pigeons."* (NRSV) This means that Mary and Joseph made an offering to God of two doves. In Leviticus 12:6-8, it explains the regulations dealing with the purification of a woman who gives birth.

First, it declares that the woman is unclean during her flow of blood, and by being "unclean" she must offer a sacrifice of a lamb. Leviticus 12:6 states, *"When the days of her purification are completed... she shall bring to the priest ... a lamb in its first year for a burnt offering, and a pigeon or a turtledove for a sin offering."* (NRSV) Leviticus 12:8 states, *"If she cannot afford a sheep, she shall take two turtledoves or two pigeons, one for a burnt offering and the other for a sin offering; and the priest shall make atonement on her behalf, and she shall be clean."* (NRSV)

Now, look again in the verse from Luke above. Mary had an offering of two doves. One for a burnt offering and the other for a <u>sin</u> offering — just like the Old Testament required. So if Mary made an offering to atone her sin, it is obvious that she had sin to be atoned. This proves, undoubtedly, that Mary <u>must</u> have sinned during her life, otherwise, it goes against the whole precept of sacrificial offering, which was sacred to the Jewish custom of that day!

The concept of the Immaculate Conception was so far from truth that it was the subject of much debate through the years. Here are quotes from four Popes who denied the "Immaculate Conception" before Pius IX proclaimed it dogma.

"The Lord Jesus Christ alone, among the sons of men was born immaculate" (Leo the First). "It belongs alone to the immaculate Lamb, to have no sin at all" (Galatious). "Jesus Christ alone was truly born Holy. Whom in order that He might overcome this condition of corruptible nature, was not conceived after the manner of men" (Gregory the Great). "Eve was produced without sin, but brought forth in sin. Mary was produced in sin, but brought forth without sin" (when she bore Jesus) (Pope Innocent III).

The church maintains that no dogma can be proclaimed without the support of Scripture **and** the unanimous consent of the church fathers. I will conclude with a quote from St. Bernard of Clairveau, one of the church fathers, "For this reason our astonishment is not small, in seeing that some of you have believed to be able to introduce a new feast. The feast of the Immaculate

Conception, that is unknown to the rights of the Holy Catholic Church, cannot be approved by reason and is condemned by all ancient tradition."

This is only one of a number of disagreements found with the church fathers. Even the tradition in the church does not support such a teaching. This being said, by its own standard, then, the Immaculate Conception shouldn't even be part of the church's doctrine.

What it does do, is strive to show Mary as sinless which only serves to equate her with Christ who was perfect and without sin.

**Step three:** Praying to Mary. "Hail, holy Queen, Mother of mercy, our life, our sweetness, and our hope, . . ." This begins one of the many prayers "honoring" Mary. It again shows far more than the simple honor Catholics profess that they give to Jesus' mother. This prayer alone is enough to prove that it is worship far more than respect that they offer her.

She is called "holy Queen", yet she was not a queen at all. Again, her position is being escalated to resemble that of Christ. Jesus Christ is the King of Kings. Mary is called the Queen of Heaven in the Catholic Church, yet again, there is no hint of evidence in Scripture or in the history of the church to indicate this notion.

Most important of all regarding this prayer is that it is a prayer offered <u>to</u> Mary. Of all the prayers I was taught in the Catholic Church, prayers to Mary far exceeded all the other prayers. In fact, more often than not, I was told to go to Mary for help if I had a problem.

In attempting to justify these prayers, the explanation is such; "to God through Mary". This is reasoned with the belief that "because Mary is Jesus' mother, she has special favor with him. Therefore, if we ask Mary to go to Him for us, she can more surely obtain our requests." This presumption is totally contrary to Biblical teaching.

To establish exactly how Jesus felt about favoritism, let us look at Luke 8:20-21. In this passage, Jesus is inside a house speaking to a large crowd, and His mother and brothers try to get in to see Him. Someone told Him, *"'Your mother and your brothers are standing outside, wanting to see you'. But he said to them, 'My mother and my brothers are those who hear the word of God and do it.'"* (NRSV) Here, Jesus gives an incredible message to us all. He distinguishes each and every believer as His own <u>mother</u> or <u>brother</u>. Does that sound like favoritism! Certainly not. In fact, Jesus affirms that He will regard me as He would His own earthly mother because I believe God's Word.

If Mary had even the slightest favor with Jesus, He would not have told us otherwise. We are all special to Jesus, and to believe that He would listen to Mary more affectionately, totally disregards Scripture.

Further study in the Bible reveals the first "worshipper" of Mary. We read in Luke 11:27-28, a passage where Jesus is again speaking to a crowd. *"While he was saying this, a woman in the crowd raised her voice and said to him, "Blessed is the womb that bore you and the breasts that nursed you!" But he said, "Blessed rather are those who hear the word of God and obey it!.'"* (NRSV) Jesus discounts this woman's praise of His mother and puts the emphasis on the more important Word of God. He shows no favor with His mother, rather He shows caution to those who direct too much attention to her.

Jesus shows by this statement that He does not want us to exalt His mother, but rather obey the Word of God. Why? Because Mary is not extraordinary when it comes to salvation. She cannot gain anything for us. We do not have any need for Mary. John 16:23-24, confirms this. Jesus tells us, *"On that day you will ask nothing of me. Very truly, I tell you, if you ask anything of the Father in my name, he will give it to you. Until now you have not asked for anything in my name. Ask and you will receive, so that your joy may be complete."* (NRSV) We do not have to go to Mary to receive what we need. Jesus tells us that through Him, we will receive. This is a direct promise from Christ Himself. He does not mention anywhere that we should go to Mary. In fact, by praying to Mary, we are only showing that we do not trust Christ to keep His promise.

Verification from Scripture is found in 1 Timothy 2:5, *"there is one God; there is also one mediator between God and humankind, Christ Jesus, himself human."* (NRSV) Here is an undeniable resolution as to Whom we are to pray. We have already determined that prayer to Mary is pointless because she has no favor with Christ. We have also confirmed that through Christ we can obtain whatever we ask. Now, by this verse, we are told that Mary <u>cannot</u> help us. In fact <u>no one</u> but Jesus Christ can be our mediator.

The Catholic Church, when faced with this verse, claimed Mary to be the "mediatrix" for us. This "female" version of the word mediator is a ridiculous attempt to get around the Bible's truth that there is only <u>one</u> intercessor. Their argument is that Jesus is the one mediator the Bible talks about, and Mary is the mediatrix. They created a new word to defend their position on this dogma.

The Bible was not written in English as we discussed in previous chapters and, therefore, we must understand what is actually being said. In the verse above, we are told that there is only <u>one</u> mediator between God and ourselves. This word mediator is translated from the Greek word "mesites" which means a "go-between" or an "intercessor". This verse clearly states that there is only <u>one</u> intercessor between God and men — Jesus Christ is that One. Mary cannot, and is not, a mediator for us; nor is she a "mediatrix". The Bible says it plainly and clearly – only one person can intercede for us to God and that is His Son, Jesus Christ.

Claiming Mary to be the "mediatrix" to whom we offer prayer only strives to equate her with Jesus, who is the only true intercessor for us.

**Step four:** Mary's assumption into heaven. This doctrine is explained in the Catechism as follows: "By a very special privilege, the body of a human person has been preserved from corruption and taken into heaven.

That person is the Blessed Virgin Mary." It continues . . . "this special privilege proclaimed a dogma of faith by Pope Pius on November 1, 1950." Here again, we see a teaching in the church that is established by a single Pope. It is claimed by him to be infallibly true and is supposed to be supported by Scripture as the church has always mandated. Once again, though, we will discover how contrary the Bible is to this doctrine.

First of all, we must recognize that there is nothing in Scripture at all to indicate that Mary ascended into Heaven. References to Mary the mother of Jesus, are found in forty eight verses. Of these, only one reference is made regarding Mary after Christ's death and resurrection. In the book of Acts, chapter 14, Mary the mother of Jesus is mentioned as one of the many disciples in the upper room. There is nothing more mentioned about her in Scripture after that.

This is the first step in verifying the error of doctrine in question. It is not proven in Scripture that it did happen, so how can we claim it to be true? In response to this question, a priest said that just because it was not mentioned, it "cannot be held as an absolute proof" that it <u>did not</u> happen!

To understand what really took place, let us look at the logical chain of events quoted in the Bible. We can begin by looking at John 19:26-27. This passage begins with Jesus hanging on the cross ready to die. He looks down and sees His mother and John, one of the apostles, standing there. *"When Jesus saw his mother and the disciple whom he loved standing beside her, he said to his mother, "Woman, here is your son." Then he said to the disciple, "Here is your mother." And from that hour the disciple took her into his own home."* (NRSV) John took Mary into his home, and as she got older, he cared for her. This was a very understandable gesture because Jesus wanted to see to the care of His mother. It is also important to note that John was a very appropriate person for the task. First of all, John had a special relationship with Jesus. John refers to himself as "the disciple that Jesus loved." This indicates that there was a very intimate friendship between them. Jesus knew John would take very good care of Mary.

Another important point is that John lived the longest of all the apostles. He would not be one to die and leave Mary to find another to care for her. Obviously, this made John an even better choice for the job. Jesus knew what He was doing. Now let us continue the chain of events. John, we recognize, has taken Mary into his home. Church historians and scholars have estimated that Mary died around 70 A.D., and John died about 90 A.D. It is a fact that John wrote his gospel just before he died. This means that John wrote his gospel approximately twenty years after Mary's death.

If there was one person on earth that would have known about Mary's "assumption", it would have been John. He was in charge of her care. He most likely would have been there or at least he would have heard first hand of such an event. So now let us look at John's own words.

In the gospel of John 3:13, John writes: *"No one has ascended into heaven except the one who descended from heaven, the Son of Man."* (NRSV) Here, John tells us as straightforward as possible, that Jesus was the <u>only</u> one to ascend into heaven. If there was any chance that Mary ascended into heaven, John would certainly have not said otherwise.

In a letter to a priest, I questioned this obviously false doctrine of the assumption, and included the above mentioned verse from Scripture. In his reply, the priest said, "no one has ascended into heaven like Jesus, is quite true, but that mere statement need not exclude a different type of going up, which was His Mother's assumption."

This statement quoted directly from a priest's letter, makes it clear how false doctrines begin. Notice his attempt to avoid proof from Scripture. He tries to make the claim that this verse "need not exclude a different" way for Mary to have gone up. He supposes that the Bible just does not say that Mary went up the "same way" Jesus did.

In his statement though, he does something that causes his downfall — he <u>changes</u> Scripture. He said that, "no one has ascended into heaven <u>like</u> Jesus, is quite true . . ." Here, he has directly misquoted Scripture to explain and support his own belief in Mary's "assumption". The Bible says in that verse, *"and no one has ascended into heaven except the one"* This constitutes a <u>single</u> person and a <u>single</u> act of ascension. There were no other ascensions. To say that Mary went up a <u>different</u> way is a vain attempt to justify this doctrine.

To prove the Bible's position that Mary could not have ascended into heaven, let us look at 1 Corinthians 15:50, *"What I am saying, brothers and sisters, is this: flesh and blood cannot inherit the kingdom of God, nor does the perishable inherit the imperishable."* (NRSV) Here we are told that only the immortal body can enter heaven. Jesus is immortal – He died and at His resurrection took on an immortal body so of course He is in heaven. Mary would have to have been immortal also to have been assumed into heaven. Recorded in 1 Timothy 6:16, *"It is he(*Christ*) alone who has immortality"* (NRSV) Here it plainly states that Christ alone was immortal and, therefore, Mary being mortal could not have ascended into heaven.

Biblical study shows, without a doubt, that Mary did not ascend into heaven bodily. Making this assumption, and then claiming it to be doctrine ordained by God, is a serious offence to Him. It also goes against the very foundations of the Catholic Church, which mandates that Scripture must support all dogma.

By claiming that Mary was assumed into heaven, the Church is trying to elevate Mary's significance to that of Jesus, who truly did ascend into heaven.

**Sept five:** Mary's perpetual virginity. Catholic teaching insists that Mary, who was a virgin before the birth of Jesus, remained a virgin throughout her life. Again, here is another attempt to make Mary appear more holy than she really was.

In the first chapter of Matthew, we read about Joseph taking Mary as his wife, and verse 25 says, *"But had no marital relations with her until she had borne a son; and he named him Jesus."* (NRSV) Joseph had no union with Mary <u>until</u> she gave birth to Jesus. The actual Greek word used here is "hoes" which is an adverb of continuance. It means that after the fact (Jesus' birth), the act (union with Mary) would have taken place.

In that culture, a marriage was considered complete after the man and woman were united in a sexual relation. Even though Mary and Joseph had gone through the ceremonies and celebrations with their family and friends, they had not had relations because Mary was pregnant. That is why the Bible points out that they did not have relations <u>until</u> Jesus was born.

To make the claim that Mary did not unite with Joseph in their marriage bond, does two things. First, it would mean that Mary did not fulfill her wifely duties, and she and Joseph were not truly united as man and wife. Secondly, by saying that Mary remained a virgin suggests that sex is somehow wrong, and that she would not have participated in anything that displeased God. Therefore, it demeans the sexual relationship in a marriage, even though it is a perfectly holy and upright act designed by God.

Furthermore, the Bible tells us that Jesus had brothers. Recorded in Luke 8:19, *"Then his mother and his brothers came to him,"* (NRSV) His <u>brothers</u> came to see Him — they were with His mother!

In Mark 6:3, we read how Jesus goes into His own land to preach. Here He is recognized by many people. After listening to Him they remark, *"Is not this the carpenter, the son of Mary and brother of James and Joses and Judas and Simon, and are not his sisters here with us?"* (NRSV) Here the Bible names His brothers. The Greek word used in this passage is "adelphos", which means literally "connected to – the womb". It is translated as "a <u>brother</u> (literally or figuratively) near or remote".

The Catholic Church argues that the word can mean "cousin" not just brother, claiming that the names given are sons of Jesus aunt and uncle. Although the translation includes the possibility of distant kin, the context of the verse does not. If we look at Matthew 13:55-56 the reference states *"Is not this the carpenter's son? Is not his mother called Mary? And are not his brothers James and Joseph and Simon and Judas? And are not all his sisters with us?"* (NRSV) Here is the same story in Matthew that we read in Mark 6 above. Jesus visits his hometown and is rejected by the people who know him. They comment on how he is the son of the carpenter and Mary and then they name his brothers. There is no sensible way to translate that these people would name the parents of the son, and then include his cousins. Why wouldn't they mention the aunt and uncle? In addition, they mention Jesus "sisters". This would be even more illogical to translate as "cousin" because if they were not His true sisters, as females, they would not be worth mentioning. That is because women were not significant in that time.

There are no passages in Scripture that use the word "adelphos" to mean cousin when the parents are named. Interpreting the word to mean distant relatives is a weak attempt to support Mary's perpetual virginity. We can conclude that Jesus was **not** an only child — He had brothers and sisters from His mother Mary and earthly father Joseph.

Alleging that Mary was a perpetual virgin only aims to place her above everyone else and make her seem more like Christ who did not unite with any woman, but remained separate, solely devoted to His ministry.

**Step six:** Titles given to Mary. There are many titles dedicated to Mary. The following list is taken from a Catholic weekly magazine called "Our Sunday Visitor", published January 27, 1962. The names mentioned are found inscribed around a crown surrounding Mary's head: "Queen of the Angels, Comforter of the Afflicted, Mother of Good Counsel, Morning Star, Gate of Heaven, House of Gold, Tower of David, Tower of Ivory, Mystical Rose, Ark of the Covenant, Health of the sick, Refuge of the sinners, Mother most Admirable, Amiable, Inviolate, Chaste, Pure, Mother of Devine Grace, Mother of Christ, Holy Virgin of Virgins, <u>Singular Vessel of Devotion</u>, <u>Holy Mother of God</u>, Holy Mary, Help of Christians, Queen Conceived without Sin, Queen of all Saints, Queen of Virgins, Queen of Confessors, Martyrs, Apostles, Prophets, Patriarchs, Queen of the most Holy Rosary, Vessel of Honor, <u>Spiritual Vessel</u>, <u>Seat of Wisdom</u>, Cause of our Joy, Mirror of Justice, <u>Virgin most Merciful</u>, <u>Powerful</u>, <u>Renowned</u>, <u>Venerable</u>, <u>Prudent</u>, Mother of our Savior, <u>Mother of our Creator</u>".

These are just a handful of the titles given to Mary by the Catholic Church. Yet, they claim that they do not worship her? Six of these titles belong exclusively to Jesus Christ.

Revelation 22:16, states, *"It is I, Jesus, who sent my angel to you with this testimony for the churches. I am the root and the descendant of David, the bright morning star."* (NRSV) Who do Catholics call their "Morning Star?" Not Jesus, as the Bible states, but Mary.

We read in John 10:9, Jesus' statement, *"I am the gate. Whoever enters by me will be saved,"* (NRSV) Jesus calls Himself the gate by which we can be saved and can enter heaven. Yet, Mary is referred to as the "Gate of Heaven". This title truly belongs to Christ alone, and is wrongly given to Mary.

Exodus 25, describes the Ark of the Covenant. It was an ark or box, especially designed by God and built by the Israelites. It carried the stone tablets on which were written the Ten Commandments, and for the

Israelites it was a direct source to God. The Catholics call Mary the "Ark of the Covenant". This is ridiculous. Mary was certainly not a wooden box. She did not carry the commandments and she is not a direct source to God.

We read in 2 Samuel 22:3, David's praise to God saying, *"my God, my rock, in whom I take refuge, my shield and the horn of my salvation, my stronghold and my refuge, my savior; you save me from violence. . . ."* (NRSV) Psalm 34:8, says, *"O taste and see that the Lord is good; happy are those who take refuge in him."* (NRSV) Psalm 118:8 says, *"It is better to take refuge in the Lord than to put confidence in mortals."* (NRSV)

The Bible calls the Lord our refuge. Catholic teaching calls Mary the "refuge of the sinners". Mary cannot save sinners and therefore, she could not possibly be their refuge. This title is totally inappropriate and gives the impression that Mary has the ability to bring us salvation.

Recorded in Exodus 20:5, is God's first commandment. It says, *"I the Lord your God am a jealous God."* (NRSV) God does not share His place of worship, yet Mary is called the "Singular Vessel of Devotion"! God does not want us giving devotion to anyone but Himself! By this title, we can see more clearly that Mary is given more than the "honor" the Catholic Church claims. If, indeed, Mary is a "singular vessel of devotion" to Catholics, then they are certainly worshipping her.

Of all the titles given to Mary, the title of Queen is, I believe, the greatest in an attempt to elevate Mary to Christ's position. Christ is called "King of Kings" in Revelation 17:14, and Mary is called "Queen of the Angels" and of "the saints" and "the apostles", etc. She is given this royal name to equate her with the role of royalty. The fact is, however, that the "royalty" belongs to God alone. For if Christ is considered King and Mary is called Queen, then she would have to be a goddess. Christ is God — Mary is not. There is no queen in God's kingdom. The Bible makes it clear that God is the only one with power, and He says Himself, that He will not share His place.

The title "Queen of Heaven" was also bestowed on Mary. This is one title that is actually found in the Bible in Jeremiah 7:18, *"The children gather wood, the fathers kindle fire, and the women knead dough, to make cakes for the queen of heaven; and they pour out drink offerings to other gods, to provoke me to anger."* (NRSV) Here we read about the "Queen of Heaven". She was a pagan goddess. This, of course, is not why the name was given to Mary, but it shows what little diligence was given to the Bible when it was chosen. And note that God was very angry with the devotion they showed to this "Queen of Heaven".

Finally, the name "Mother of Our Creator" was given to Mary. This is much like the title "Mother of God". The body of Jesus did not create the universe. Mary did not exist when the universe was created. The

Creator is the Almighty God who consists of the Father, Son and the Holy Spirit. Jesus has always existed, but His physical body did not. Mary bore the physical body of Jesus – she did not bear God the Trinity, nor did she give birth to the deity of Jesus. The act of birth is the beginning of human life. The deity of Jesus is eternal and was not created in Mary.

The Mary of the Bible and the Mary of the Catholic Church are two very different women. The following quote given by Pope Pius 12th in 1950, clearly discloses the Mary of Catholicism.

"Enraptured by the splendor of your heavenly beauty and impelled by the anxieties of the world, we cast ourselves into your arms. Oh Immaculate Mother of Jesus and our Mother Mary, confident of finding in your most loving heart the appeasement of our ardent desires and the safe harbor from the tempests which beset us on every side. Though degraded by our faults and overwhelmed by infinite misery, we admire and praise the peerless richness of this sublime gift which God has filled you above every mere creature from the first moment of your conception until the day on which after your assumption into heaven, He crowned you queen of the universe. Oh Crystal Fountain of Faith, Oh Fragrant Lily of all Holiness, capture our hearts with your heavenly perfume. Oh Conqueress of Evil and Death, inspire in us a deep horror of sin which makes the soul detestable to God and a slave of hell. Oh well beloved of God, hear the ardent cry which rises up from every heart in this year dedicated to you. Bend tenderly over our aching wounds. Convert the wicked, dry the tears of the afflicted and oppressed, comfort the poor and humble, quench hatred, sweeten harshness, safeguard the flower of purity in youth, and protect the Holy Church. Make all men feel the attraction of Christian goodness. In your name resounding harmoniously in heaven may they recognize that they are brothers, and the nations are members of one family upon which may there shine forth the Son of the universal and sincere peace. Receive oh most sweet mother, our humble supplications and above all, obtain for us that on that day, happy with you we may repeat <u>before your throne</u> that hymn which is today sung, earth around your <u>altars</u>. You are all beautiful oh Mary, you are the glory, you are the honor, you are the joy of the people. Amen".

This is a perfect testimony of worship to Mary. Note again, where it says, "cast ourselves into your arms" and "before your throne" and "around your altars". Mary does not have a throne in heaven. Giving the impression that she does, only falsely elevates her position; and claiming that she has an altar, goes even further. An altar is used to make sacrifices to God. Is Mary considered a goddess? This confirms the worship of Mary in the Catholic Church. And remember, this was said by a Pope!

Catholicism promotes the worship of Mary. The Church claims that Mary is "venerated" not worshipped.

But in addition to their already mentioned excuses, they argue that, "How can God disprove of the praise of His masterpiece?" I read an article in a Catholic monthly newsletter called the "Marion Helper", which is published by a Catholic organization devoted to the mother of Jesus. The author compared God to an artist and Mary to the greatest of His works of art. In the article, the writer talked of this masterpiece of God and how, by praising the masterpiece, we show praise to the One who created the masterpiece.

If we believe this concept that Mary is God's "masterpiece", then we defy the one principle in the Bible that will never change. The Word of God is the perfect source of truth. The Catholic Church teaches the authenticity of God's Word and claims that no doctrine will be made dogma unless it is backed by Holy Scripture. In Romans 1:25, we are told what the truth really is regarding the "praise' of God's created "masterpiece": *"They exchanged the truth about God for a lie and worshiped and served the creature rather than the Creator, who is blessed forever. Amen."* (NRSV) God does not want us to devote our attention to any creature, including Mary. For she was created just like us, and when we give her more honor than the One who created her - we "exchange the truth of God for a lie"!

God's true "Masterpiece" is His own Son. Jesus Christ is the One and <u>only</u> One who deserves our utmost praise and honor. To be truly devoted to Him, we <u>cannot</u>

give honor to someone else. This would only take away from the commitment we have to Him. To claim that because Mary was Jesus' mother, He is honored by our praise of her, is a lie of the devil.

**Step seven:** The last of the Catholic "steps to deity" of Mary is their making her the "Co-redemptrix". This is again a "female" version of the word redeemer. Christ is our redeemer, we read in the book of Romans 3:23-24, *"since all have sinned and fall short of the glory of God; they are now justified by his grace as a gift, through the redemption that is in Christ Jesus."* (NRSV) There is only one redeemer and that is Christ Jesus.

The Catholic Church teaches that Mary is the "co-redemptrix" which supposes that Mary "helped" Jesus redeem us. This, therefore, infers that she is responsible, in part, for our salvation.

First and foremost, Mary did not take part in the actual redemption process. Jesus' death and resurrection was the means for our salvation and Mary took no part in either. She did not die on the cross, and was not raised from the dead with Him. Mary's only role in the story of Christ is her giving birth to Jesus.

Mary was Jesus' mother. She was used of God to bear the physical body of Jesus. For this reason, she should be honored, but she cannot be considered a "co-savior" with Christ. She too was in need of a savior. So how could she have possibly been responsible, even in part, for our salvation?

The fact is, Jesus did not need any help in redeeming

us. He is fully capable as God to bring us to salvation on His own — and that is just what he did. As Christians, we can rely on Jesus Christ <u>alone</u> to save us from our sin. Catholic teaching, however, presumes another "way" of salvation in addition to Christ.

The following quote by Cardinal Spellman reveals how much Mary has become the "savior", even beyond that of Jesus. It states, <u>"Oh Mary, Gate of Heaven, none shall enter in except through thee"</u>. What he is in fact saying is that Mary is the way to heaven, and that we must go through her to get there. We read in John 14:6, Jesus' words, *"I am the way, and the truth, and the life. No one comes to the Father except through me."* (NRSV) Jesus makes a very different claim - not through Mary, but through Christ are we saved!

There are many Catholics who may disagree with me in regard to the claim that Mary is considered a "co-redeemer" by the Catholic Church. The fact is, however, that this is what the church teaches and promotes. The following quotes are taken from a prayer book called "Visits to the Most Blessed Sacrament and the Blessed Virgin Mary". These quotes establish the Catholic teaching on the subject of Mary's "saving power".

The prayers to Mary were written by St. Alphonsus Liguori. Because they are numerous, I have only used the phrases that were most relevant to the issue at hand. "Oh great Queen, I thank you . . . particularly for <u>having delivered me from hell</u>, . . . I promise to serve you always, . . . I confined my salvation to your care, and since you are so powerful with God, deliver me from all temptations, . . . until you see me safe in heaven, . . . signing your mercies for all eternity. I am a miserable sinner who turns to you, refuge of sinners, please help me. My Lady, if you do not help me, I am lost . . . I place all my trust in you. You are the reason for my hope. You must save me too! You see to the salvation of everyone who perseveres in praying to you. Be my hope of salvation. Where shall I turn if you reject me? To ignore you could endanger my salvation. I make myself your slave. You can still save me . . . my Mother you must save me! I kneel at your feet hoping you will obtain pardon for me. Only those souls who fail to see your help eventually find themselves in hell. She is a lifeboat that will save us from the shipwreck of eternal damnation. You are the one who guides souls to God. Let me be your faithful servant till death."

This is the Mary of Catholicism. A "savior" whom they serve, not the Mary of the Bible who Jesus spoke of in Luke 11:28, *"He replied, "Blessed rather are those who hear the word of God and obey it'."* (NRSV) This was in response to the woman who said *"Blessed is the womb that bore you."* (NRSV) (Luke 11:27) I am repeating this verse from Scripture because it clearly defines who Jesus wants us to devote ourselves to. God alone in the persons of the Trinity is worthy of all our devotion.

To review, here again are the seven steps that try to equate Mary to Jesus;

1: The Bible teaches that Jesus is the Son of God, Catholic teaching suggests that Mary is the Mother of God

2: The Bible teaches that Jesus alone was sinless, Catholic teaching says that Mary had an immaculate conception.

3: The Bible teaches that Jesus is our single mediator between God and men, Catholic teaching claims that Mary is our mediatrix.

4: The Bible teaches that Christ alone ascended into heaven, Catholic teaching assumes that Mary was "assumed" into heaven.

5: The Bible teaches that Jesus did not marry, but remained separate during His earthly life, Catholic teaching alleges that Mary remained a virgin throughout her life.

6: The Bible bestows many titles to Jesus, including King of kings, Catholic teaching assigns many titles to Mary, including Queen

7: The Bible declares Jesus the One and only Redeemer, Catholic teaching asserts that Mary is the co-redemtrix

In conclusion, I feel I must address briefly, the claim that Mary has appeared on numerous occasions to various people, i.e., at Lourdes and Fatima, etc. The fact is that Mary died a normal death, and did not "assume" bodily into heaven, as we have already proven in this chapter. However, to say that the visions of Mary's appearances were all lies or hallucinations would be unfair. There is a very reasonable explanation for these sightings and it is found in 2 Corinthians 11:14, *"And no wonder! Even Satan disguises himself as an angel of light."* (NRSV) Isn't this precisely how the visions of Mary are described? She appeared to each one as an "angel of light". This description of her is seen in the artwork of those who have painted portraits of the "Lady of Fatima".

These are the words of Sister Lucia, the woman who as a young girl, witnessed a series of "visions" of Mary. This is quoted from the booklet <u>Lucia Speaks on the Message of Fatima</u>. Here she describes the "apparitions" of Mary: ". . . we beheld a beautiful lady dressed in white. She was more brilliant than the sun, radiating a sparkling light." This is a perfect picture of the "angel of light" spoken of in God's word.

The only way we can be sure something is from God is to use His Word as our guide. We read in 1 John 4:1, *"Beloved, do not believe every spirit, but test the spirits to see whether they are from God; for many false prophets have gone out into the world."* (NRSV) We have already proven with Scripture, that the claims made about Mary are totally contradictory to Scripture. That being true then, the "appearances" of Mary have to be the tricks of Satan.

In addition to these "appearances", some would argue that there were "healings" that have come about at the locations of the sightings. They call these "miracles" proof that the "appearances" really were from God.

We know that Satan wants these "appearances" to be believed so he will do anything in his power to deceive us. Therefore we can be certain that the so called "healings" are his work also.

Satan has the power to inflict illness and injury on us, and likewise he can remove the same. Read the book of Job and see where Satan plagued Job with many terrible things. If he can benefit from removing illness to make us think it is a healing, then he is willing to do so. In fact, I believe Satan has inflicted many people for that very purpose – to withdraw the illness in order to mislead them into giving false devotion.

We <u>must</u> constantly *"test the spirits"* as the Bible says to be sure that they are of God. To believe and accept the words of men when they are explicitly against God's Word is deplorable. These visions prove all the more how detrimental the church's elevation of Mary is. If the church had taught the Biblical perspective of Mary, then Satan would have had a much harder time convincing people with these false appearances.

Throughout the Bible we read how God wants our focus to be on Him. God **never** asked us to go to Mary to intercede and doing so only causes a separation between us and God. Catholic doctrine has overtly put the focus on Mary in the Catholic's life and for many Catholics it has created a disconnection in their relationship with God.

God the Father sent His Son, His One and only Son, Jesus Christ, to earth as a human being. **This** is the person we should devote **all** our attention to. Jesus became human so we could have a personal relationship to Him, as God. There is **no** other human being worthy of our praise, honor or prayers.

# – 11 –

# Tradition

In this final chapter, I wish to examine the topic of tradition. The Catholic Church bases much of its doctrine on tradition, and so a thorough examination of the authenticity of tradition is essential.

First of all, what is tradition? The Catholic Church describes it as being the "unwritten Word of God". It also states that "Sacred Tradition" is just as important as the Bible. This is said because in the beginning, the Christian Church did not have the written Word. In fact, the Bible itself, that is, the New Testament, was not formed into a book until the second century after Christ's death.

The New Testament of the Bible is a series of 27 books written over a period of 60 to 80 years. During that time, the apostles wrote letters to the newly formed churches throughout the land. These inspired letters were circulated within the churches for the teaching of the Gospel. By the second century, the church gathered the writings of the apostles and put together the first New Testament. However, up until that time, the churches depended on the spoken words of the apostles as their guide. There was no New Testament for them to refer to. Yet, they studied their own Scripture, the Old Testament, to confirm what they were being taught was God's will. They corroborated what they were being taught with what Old Testament Scripture said.

All in all, the "tradition" that was depended upon was the teaching of those who were first-hand witnesses of Christ. This included the original apostles and Paul, who was converted after Christ's death and resurrection. Before the Word was actually written down, Christians had to follow the actions and beliefs of those who taught about Jesus. Later, the written Word was used as the teaching guide for Christians.

When we look at this as the basic explanation for "tradition", it is quite acceptable that tradition be of great value to the Christian Church. However, Catholicism teaches that tradition has continued throughout the centuries even after the New Testament was complete.

This is made apparent in the development of the "Immaculate Conception" of Mary. This doctrine was established as dogma in 1854, but began in the 700's. The following explanation is lengthy; but please understand that it is necessary to follow through the whole process of how "tradition" plays a role in the Catholic church. This is the history of the "Immaculate Conception" as told in the book, "Fundamentals of Catholic Dogma". "Since the seventh century, a Feast of the Conception of St. Anne . . . was celebrated. The object of the celebration of the feast was initially the active conception of St. Anne." Here is where it all began. In the 700's, people began celebrating a day dedicated to the conception of Mary, in her mother St. Anne. This beginning was not the Immaculate Conception of today. It was strictly a feast celebrating the conception of Mary, not of her "sinless beginning".

The book continues, "At the beginning of the twelfth century, the British monk Eadmer . . . advocated the Immaculate Conception of Mary, that is, her conception free from original sin. Eadmer wrote the first monograph on this subject." Now we see where the doctrine began. The monk Eadmer began promoting the idea by encouraging the belief that Mary was sinless. He did not base his presumption on Scripture. In fact, the book continues, "On the other hand, St. Bernard of Clairvaux, warned the faithful that this was an unfounded innovation . . . Under the influence of St. Bernard, the leading theologians of the twelfth and thirteenth centuries rejected the doctrine of the Immaculate Conception."

The true history of this doctrine is that it was introduced as a church precept, by a monk, eleven hundred years after the apostles were dead, and after the Bible was already formed. In addition to that, the top theologians of that time denied the possibility of such a theory. And St. Bernard a "Church Father" warned against such a doctrine. Yet, the church maintains that "tradition" supports this doctrine!

In the book, the history behind this dogma continues. It states of the theologians and St. Bernard that, "Their difficulty was that they had not yet found the way to bring Mary's freedom from original sin into consonance with the universality of original sin, and with the necessity of all men for redemption." The book claims that the church fathers were having a hard time accepting the idea because they couldn't "yet" explain how it happened.

The fact is that these men could not reconcile such a belief with Scripture. They knew that tradition never taught such a concept, and they wholeheartedly disagreed with it. St. Bernard said the new feast "cannot be approved by reason, and is condemned by all ancient tradition."

Yet, the church states that these men "had not yet found the way".

The theologians of that day and the Church Fathers were beyond the time of "tradition". Tradition was founded in the teachings of the apostles. The apostolic teaching was then transformed into the Bible's New Testament. From then on, the young Christian church analyzed each new idea with beliefs taught in the Scripture. In the twelfth century, the tradition of the Christian church was already established. The doctrine of the "Immaculate Conception" was not part of that tradition. But the Catholic Church claims that tradition is where it is validated. The truth is, the doctrine of the Immaculate Conception was a presumption advocated by a monk without the support of Scripture or tradition.

The book goes on to say that the "problem" that faced St. Bernard was finally "solved" by a man named John Duns Scotus. He claimed that Mary was, indeed, redeemed, but this redemption took place "before" she was born, and in a "special" way! Even this theory was not "taken from" Scripture. Instead, it was "fit into" Scripture by using the verses from Genesis 3, to claim that Mary was somehow "implied" in the passage. The book states "The doctrine of the Immaculate Conception of Mary is not explicitly revealed in Scripture . . . it is contained implicitly in the following passages: "Genesis 3:15, *"I will put enmity between you and the woman, and between thy seed and her seed. He* (seed of the woman) *shall crush thy head, and thou shall crush his heel."* The book continues its explanation, "The literal sense of the passage is possibly the following: ..." It goes on to manipulate Scripture to fit their belief, and it is proclaimed a dogma in 1854 (discussed in Chapter Ten of this book).

This is the basis for "tradition" in the Catholic Church. To follow through it again; first, people began a "feast" for Mary's mother, and then a monk promoted the claim that Mary was conceived without sin. The top theologians totally disagreed with it, but another man came along hundreds of years later and gave an idea as to how it "could" have happened. And finally, the passage of Scripture that seemed most "fitting" was used to justify the belief "implicitly". All this occurred over a period of 1100 years.

The "tradition" that the above doctrine is based on is "human tradition". It began with ordinary people, and it was not reconciled with God's Word. It is not the same tradition that was established by the apostles. Their teaching always agreed with the Scripture, but above all, the beliefs of the early church were taken from what they were taught. They did not come up with a belief and then try to make Scripture agree with it.

God is a wise and perfect God. He does not contradict Himself. It would go against His nature to change. Malachi 3:6 states, *"I the Lord do not change."* (NRSV) With this in mind, all tradition that goes against God's Word cannot be from God – it is impossible.

In an interview with a priest, I asked if tradition and Scripture were to contradict, then what should be believed. He replied that they could not disagree, but that the "trouble" with the Bible is that it is a lifelong study in order to get anything out of it. He claimed that tradition is just as important as Scripture, but easier to follow.

This theory is ridiculous when you consider that tradition in the Catholic Church includes beliefs that surfaced long after the Bible was <u>complete</u>. In fact, making such a statement causes those who accept it to depend on others for what to believe. This, of course, is what the Catholic Church expects.

The Catholic Church teaches that they are the only true source of interpretation for the Bible, and that it is through them that one can come to understand God's Word. This quote from the book "Catholicism" explains what the church contends. "Catholic theologians maintain that as a source of truth, tradition is superior to Scripture. Scripture is, after all, incomplete. It not only requires interpretation, but it required tradition in order that it might be recognized and established."

This proposal is a very serious step in the <u>wrong</u> direction. This belief leads to the notion that God's Word is not perfect! That, of course is blasphemous. What the Catholic Church is trying to declare is that there is more truth than what the Bible contains and that tradition is a continuation of God's divine revelation.

If this belief was truly from God, His Word could not dispute it. The truth is that God's Word is <u>complete</u>. Adopting any doctrine that is not "explicitly" passed on by Scripture is adding to God's Word. The Bible is very clear about this error. It states in Revelation 22:18, *"I warn everyone who hears the words of the prophecy of this book: if anyone adds to them, God will add to that person the plagues described in this book."* (NRSV) The Word of God is sufficient in and of itself. Tradition is beneficial <u>only</u> when it is in agreement with Scripture. With that in mind, can we find anywhere in Scripture the explicit revelation that Mary was without sin? No! Nor do we find any proof in God's Word that the other doctrines mentioned in this book are from Him. In fact, all of the doctrines mentioned explicitly contradict Scripture.

Tradition, therefore, has become the route through which the Catholic Church has established many of their false doctrines. The tradition they have depended on, however, is the human tradition we examined earlier in this chapter. The apostle Paul knew the danger of human tradition. In Colossians 2:8, he says *"See to it that no one takes you captive through philosophy and empty deceit, according to human tradition, according to the elemental spirits of the universe, and not according to Christ."* (NRSV) The doctrines I have mentioned depend on the traditions and the theories of men. They are not of God, and cannot be validated with His Holy Scripture.

Throughout my research of the Catholic doctrines and dogmas, I have found the word "tradition" used repeatedly. The tradition of this church, however, is not at all the same tradition laid down by the apostles and their followers.

When the truth about an issue is to be verified, it must be found in Scripture first. Catholicism, however, has taken concepts derived from men and interpreted the Bible to "fit" those beliefs. Human tradition changes with the times, unlike God Who never changes. By using the traditions of man, the Catholic Church has instituted doctrines that conform to a sinful society.

In Acts 17:11 we are told about a group of believers from Berea. *"These Jews were more receptive than those in*

*Thessalonica, for they welcomed the message very eagerly and <u>examined the scriptures every day to see whether these things were so</u>."* (NRSV) These Bereans were called more noble because they studied the Scriptures to make sure that what the disciples had taught them was true. 2 Timothy 3:16-17 states, *"All scripture is inspired by God and is useful for teaching, for reproof, for correction, and for training in righteousness, so that everyone who belongs to God may be proficient, equipped for every good work."* (NRSV)

We are commanded in God's Word to take everything we are taught and make sure it agrees with the Bible. We should not submit to the doctrines of men, accepting what they teach us as truth, without using the Source of Truth(Bible) to validate them. God knew that men would come and try to deceive His church and so He gave us a security measure in His Word. There are many cults in the world today that are a result of people blindly following others to their own destruction.

In Acts 20:30 we read; *"Some even from your own group will come distorting the truth in order to entice the disciples to follow them."* (NRSV) And Jesus said in Matthew 7:15; *"Beware of false prophets, who come to you in sheep's clothing but inwardly are ravenous wolves."* (NRSV)

So how do we know whether or not we are being deceived? Jesus, in His great prayer to the Father for all believers, said *"Sanctify them in the truth; your word is truth."* (NRSV) (John 17:17) and Psalm 119:160 says;

*"The sum of your word is truth, and every one of your righteous ordinances endures forever."* (NRSV) The Bible is the absolute truth of God and 2 Timothy 2:15 tells us to *"Do your best to present yourself to God as one approved by him, a worker who has no need to be ashamed, rightly explaining the word of truth.."* (NRSV) "Do your best" is the Greek word "spoudazo" which means to diligently study and "rightly explaining" is the Greek word "orthotomeo" which is to correctly divide or handle the message of the Word. God gave the Word of Truth to all of us. We **all** need to study it and receive from it what God proclaims.

In summing up we can see that God warned us about those who would deceive us with false doctrines from human traditions. But He doesn't leave us hanging, He tells us to use His Holy Scripture, the Bible, to test every doctrine. The Catholic Church purports that the Bible is harder to follow than "tradition" and that we are just an "uneducated multitude" in need of the church to tell us what is right. In contrast, God tells us to study His Word so that we will not be mislead. We can understand His Word when we accept Jesus because He gives us the Holy Spirit, Who helps us comprehend it.

# Conclusion

In closing, I want to first assure you that I have a great love for Catholics. My intention is not to condemn, but to enlighten. I have found the truth in God's Word. You can find the same.

Many Catholics respond to Bible-study by saying that they have, "read it, but cannot understand it." To those who agree with this, I will direct you to 1 Corinthians 2:14 which states, *"Those who are unspiritual do not receive the gifts of God's Spirit, for they are foolishness to them, and they are unable to understand them because they are spiritually discerned."* (NRSV) Simply put, this statement says that without the Spirit, a man will not understand the Bible. The reason is logical – the Christian has the Holy Spirit, Who interprets the Word of God for him. Read Chapter Three again to learn about why Jesus sent the Holy Spirit.

Many Catholics believe that they are Christians. As a child in a Catholic school, I was always taught that I was a Christian; however, I have discovered that the meaning of Christian from a Catholic's view is very different from that found in the Bible.

The Catholic Church does profess the Lord Jesus Christ, and so considers itself to be a Christian religion. However, there is much more to being a Christian than

111

belonging to a "Christian" church. Being a Catholic <u>does</u> <u>not</u> make you a Christian, because by being a Catholic you are <u>not</u> saved! The fact is, there is only <u>one</u> way to be <u>saved</u>, and being saved is what being a Christian is all about.

I cannot stress this fact enough; that without Jesus Christ as your personal Savior, you <u>cannot</u> enter into God's kingdom. I can make no judgment against you. I am like you, a sinner. But as a Christian, I have the blood of Jesus' sacrifice covering me. This sacrifice paid, in full, the penalty of my sin. With Christ as my Savior, I can enter God's kingdom freely.

This has all been made clear in the Bible, but before you can truly understand it, you must make an honest effort to seek God's will. If you have been searching, then now is a good time to make a sincere commitment to Him. If you believe Jesus died on the cross and rose again, and is now in heaven, then you are prepared.

First, you must admit to Him that you are a sinner. By recognizing this fact, you are more able to repent from the sin in your life. Second, tell Jesus that you want to turn away from sin and accept His sacrifice as payment for it. Third, ask Jesus to come into your life and be your Savior and Lord. This means that you will put Christ first in your life.

If you do these three things, you will be opening the door of your life to Christ. This will, I promise, give you the greatest peace you will ever know. It will also bring a tremendous change to your life. 2 Corinthians

5:17 states, *"So if anyone is in Christ, there is a new creation: everything old has passed away; see, everything has become new!"* (NRSV)

This is a sample prayer that represents the above: "Dear Lord Jesus, I admit to you that I am a sinner. I believe that you died to pay for my sins. I now want to turn away from sin and make you Lord of my life. Please come into my heart. Amen."

If you faithfully say this prayer and make a genuine commitment to Jesus, then you will become a "true" Christian. That does not mean you will suddenly stop sinning, but you will have the power of the Holy Spirit to win over temptation.

It also means that you will have the Spirit's guidance in reading God's Word. And it is God's Word that will teach you the truth. That is why it is so important to read the Bible. The apostle Paul knew the importance of Bible-study. He says in Philippians 1:9-10, *"And this is my prayer, that your love may overflow more and more with knowledge and full insight to help you to determine what is best, so that in the day of Christ you may be pure and blameless."* (NRSV) Paul knew that in order to discern what is best, we have to know what is right. God's will is expressed in His Word. Paul wanted these believers to be wise and knowledgeable in their faith. In the same way, I want to encourage you to challenge your beliefs. Ask yourself why you believe what you do, and then test it with God's Word. Recorded in 1 John 4:1, is the following; *"Beloved, do not believe every spirit, but test the spirits to see whether they are from God; for many false prophets have gone out into the world."* (NRSV) And, 1 Thessalonians 5:21, tells us to *"Test everything; hold fast to what is good."* (NRSV)

As a Catholic, you are told to comply with church authority. This authority, in turn, dictates to you their interpretation of God's divine revelation. The church expects you to believe that what they teach is from God.

I have spent a lot of time researching the Bible and the doctrines of the Catholic Church. I do not expect everyone who reads this to accept it, or like it. The fact is, I sincerely want the truth to be known to all Catholics, for it is in this truth that you will be set free – free from sin and the judgment it brings.

As I end, my prayer is that God will reveal His Holy Truth to you, and that He will guide you in making an honest commitment to Him. God bless you!

# Bibliography

Basic Catechism, Daughters of
St. Paul, Boston, MA, 1982

Fundamentals of Catholic Dogma;
Ludwig Ott, B. Herder Book Co., 1955

Catholicism, George Brantl,
George Braziller, Inc., NY, 1962

Lucia Speaks on the Message of Fatima,
printed by Ave Maria Institute, Washington, NJ, 1968

The Marian Helper Magazine,
The Association of the Marian Helpers,
Stockbridge, MA

The Mystery of the Eucharist,
Max Thurian, William Eerdmans Publishing Co.,
Grand Rapids, MI ,1981

Strong's Hebrew and Greek Dictionaries, James
Strong, John R. Kohlenberger III, James A. Swanson,
Zondervan; Revised edition (September 6, 2001)

Sainthood in Roman Catholicism-What Is a
Saint-The Roman Catholic Understanding
of Sainthood, http://catholicism.about.com/
od/thesaints/f/What_Is_A_Saint.htm

Catholic Online, http://www.catholic.org/saints/
faq.php#exactly-how-many-saints-are-there

Printed in the United States
By Bookmasters